AMERICA AWAKES

BY JAN FARRINGTON

a new appraisal of the Twenties

Westover
Publishing Company

an affiliate of Media General, Richmond, Virginia

FOR Jerry and for Jackie who taught me—
For James Hopkins, great composer and greater friend—
And for Bobby Short who, in a frequently dismal world,
assures me that the game is worth the candle.
With respect, affection and gratitude.

My thanks to the staff of Firestone Library, Princeton University, for cooperation and assistance. Particular appreciation is due Miss Mary Ann Jensen, Curator of the Theatre Collection, whose patience is unending and who has worked long hours to help me in my research.

JF
June, 1971

TABLE OF CONTENTS

PREFACE

It is impossible thoroughly to examine any decade in one, small volume. Working within this limitation, I have tried to show how some men, some women, and some events were powerful forces in the shaping of the Twenties. Their shadows are long and reach on into our own times.

I did not know the Twenties but even as a child I formed an impression—aided by the glamorizing movies—of what seemed to be a decade of unmarred glory. My vision was limited. The music, show business, and literary achievements of that earlier time were all that mattered in the insular world of my youth. In these areas, the Twenties have not been equalled, before or since.

Today, I am a cop-out from that all-encompassing devotion. Although I still love the Twenties, I can see the contradictions, the inequities, the excesses of the era in a way which eluded and deluded me as a child. Yet, I still adore the plays and lyrics of Noel Coward, relish the cynicism of Sinclair Lewis, revel in the fearless iconoclasm of H. L. Mencken. In what I hope is maturity, I believe myself, as all of us, not a product of my times alone but also of the years that have gone before.

By all means, let us do our own things and, at the same time, let us encourage our children to do those things which are uniquely theirs. But in the tolerance which all older generations must adopt in order to survive, if not to prosper, let us not disparage the well-turned phrase, the facile lyric, the melodic melody, the plays and stories built upon the logic of beginning, middle and end.

Inflexibility, in thought or action, is stifling. Yet the best is not necessarily yet to come—not all of the best—and everything that passes from public fancy is not archaic and therefore worthy of the garbage heap.

Emotions that Willa Cather and Scott Fitzgerald put into words are still with us. The smash success of *Love Story* tells us that romance is still alive, albeit clouded in the four-letter vernacular of the day. For wisdom is an accumulative virtue, each poet or philosopher building upon, or tearing down and then building upon, that which came before. It is doubtful that the now accepted modes of art, music, literature, sexual behavior, international relations, or even the peace movement—to say nothing of the increasing independence of black Americans—could have come about without the revolutionary visions of the Twenties.

I have found a home in the Jazz Age which I hope you will share with me. I respect the irreverence of Dorothy Parker, the music of Jerome Kern, the flagrant innocence of Jimmy Walker, the commitment of Clarence Darrow—a commitment to the brotherhood of man which he espoused long before such commitment was popular or socially acceptable. When Darrow spoke out, radical chic was forty years in the future.

Without the contributions of these and many others, my world, for all of its flaws and distortions, would be a less rewarding place than that in which I live.

So, I believe, would it be for you.

Jan Farrington
Princeton, New Jersey
April, 1971

A Chicken *for* Every Pot

The Age of Transition:
A Hip-Pocket Summary of a Decade

The years between the end of the Great War and the coming of the Great Depression were marked by tumult and confusion. Their ups, their downs, their seemingly irreconcilable contradictions, made them much like the times in which we are living today.

As the United States reeled under its new, unwanted responsibilities as a world power, and as a superficially sound economy grew increasingly precarious, Middle America walked through life with blinders on its eyes. Most people accepted the cliché that they had "never had it so good"—even as their actions belied their words. This was a restless, frenetic society, engaged in re-examination of traditional Victorian values, enjoying a prosperity which was studded by pockets of poverty and squalor. This was a country beset by racial inequities, engaged in a conflict between the increasingly worldly and sophisticated life style of the urban centers and the ancient fundamentalism evidenced by the enormous grass-roots popularity of such evangelists as Aimee Semple McPherson and Billy Sunday.

The hinterland was trying desperately to preserve the "Faith of our Fathers" living still, despite the forces of reason which were screaming to be heard. In no single phenomenon of those years was this conflict summed up so succinctly as in that "noble experiment," Prohibition—the master pro's version of the shell game.

Even as in our own time, the Twenties gave birth to a generation gap, in part because of the new awareness of the returning doughboy ("How You Goin' To Keep Them Down on the Farm After They've Seen Paree?" queried a currently popular song). The tune was light and cheerful but the question reflected an unidentified sense of dread. The young were asking questions that their parents could not answer. Parents who believed it necessary to keep up with their children tried, out of desperation, perhaps, to imitate them.

The rift was augmented by the increasing emancipation of women, which reached a pinnacle with their achievement of the right to vote in the first year of the decade.

Prior to World War I, the woman's place was in her home and, except for the members of such organizations as the "radical" Lucy Stone League, a forerunner of Women's Lib, few thought to question the premise.

But the times were changing. Even after Woodrow Wilson failed to make the United States an integral force within his cherished League of Nations, even after the election of Warren Gamaliel Harding (a public "Dry" and a private "Wet") on the somewhat dubious platform of sobriety and a "Return to Normalcy," the forces of change could not be averted. Youth would have its day.

Morés were so altered that an admission of atheism was no longer considered shocking—not, at least, within the intellectual circles flourishing in the larger cities. Nor was it particularly daring to confess to agnosticism on most American college campuses, where many students were not committed to any creed or point of view. The clergy itself came under suspicion after Sinclair Lewis told all in *Elmer Gantry,* a novel about a rather seamy side of the religious life which deflated the hypocrisy of the Protestant ethic.

Psychiatry and psychiatrists were beginning to take the place of religion and the clergy. The names Sigmund Freud, Alfred Adler and Carl Jung were part of every educated household, although some of the concepts propounded by those gentlemen were only partially understood in an atmosphere of psychoanalytic naïveté.

Ideas, including those of sex and sexuality, were freely exchanged between men and women—for the first time in generations—and not only within the confines of the marital bedroom. Even the grand piano was acknowledged to have "legs," not "limbs," as had been the tradition in genteel conversation.

It was the era of "The Beautiful and the Damned" and its exponents were Francis Scott Key Fitzgerald, Edna St. Vincent Millay, and Dorothy Rothschild Parker—damned and beautiful all.

Sinclair Lewis was a Minnesota farm boy, slated to become a Nobel Laureate some years later. He held up a mirror to the narrow-minded intellectual sterility of Middle America through such bitter, penetrating books as *Main Street* and *Babbitt.* Those who bought his books and made him wealthy may not have liked the pictures recorded of themselves. Yet there was, even among the people who thought they understood Lewis's message of impending disaster, a nationwide obsession with pleasure—and hedonism is a pursuit which by definition encourages the superficial and non-productive.

The woman who had a few short years before averted her face as she passed the corner saloon, was now frequenting the Speak-easies and learning to "hold her liquor like a man."

Scott Fitzgerald, that tormented Princetonian, drew the country's attention to the college generation, a significantly larger group than it had been in former years as American parents became enamored of the concept of Upward Mobility.

These college-age young people were pleasure-oriented, in contrast to the austerity and political radicalism of the 30's, the apathy and complacency of the 40's and 50's (interrupted as those decades were with the tragedies of two wars) and the sense of commitment to a better world which is a hallmark of today.

Rebellion from Puritanism was in the wind, and although most people believed, or purported to believe, that the "War to End Wars" had been fought and won, that the world was "Safe for Democracy" for the next several millennia, only an undercurrent of anxiety and fear could have led to the excesses which prevailed.

The college man with his ukelele was a national hero. The co-ed, and her counterpart in shop or office, bobbed her hair, shortened her skirts, rolled down her stockings. She danced the Charleston. She drank a good deal—how much better the wine fermented from forbidden fruit! Most revolutionary of all, she experienced a degree of sexual freedom unthought of by her mother or her grandmother, a sexual freedom brought about in large part by the increasing availability of the automobile.

The duenna was dead, perhaps forever, because the rumble seat was better designed for a couple than a threesome. Most of these worthy lady chaperones enjoyed their comfort as zealously as they had protected their charges' virtue. They didn't relish overseeing the morality of the Twenties from a precarious perch on the running board of a flivver.

The boxy raccoon coat was the status symbol, and goldfish swallowing was a national pastime—although the fastidious often swallowed carrots carved to look like the fish. Inanities such as "Collegiate," having nothing whatever to do with obtaining an education, and "Yes, We Have No Bananas" topped the lists of popular songs.

Among many of the youngsters exposed to the intellectual smorgasbord of higher education, learning could not compete with the fun of the moment. It is doubtful that the parents of the "Lost Generation" had saved and sacrificed for the particular brand of academic life their children were experiencing.

H. L. Mencken's incisive magazine, *American Mercury,* was said to be on the coffee table of every fraternity house in the United States, yet one can reasonably assume that, with the exception of student "Bohemians," clustered principally in such urban academies as New York

University and the University of Chicago, few bothered to read it. The average young American was too occupied with having a good time to waste his energies on soul-searching.

As rural America tried, with some success, to ignore the cultural revolution, some of the more thoughtful and talented citizens sought to find sanity elsewhere. Caught up between the free-wheeling cult of youth and an older generation unwilling, or unable, to cast aside its outworn thinking, artists such as Gertrude Stein, Ernest Hemingway and, in time, Fitzgerald and Lewis turned to Europe, especially to Paris, where they gathered in cafes or in the salons of Miss Sylvia Beach and others to drink (legally), discuss, deplore and dream.

> While the war-induced balance of payments with Europe was working toward the collapse of the American economy;

> . . . while dust and flood were driving migrant workers from their already inadequate homes and into starvation;

> . . . while the Ku Klux Klan was enjoying prominence unknown since Reconstruction (and, yes, their crosses burn again today);

> . . . while a Dayton, Tennessee school teacher was being persecuted for the teaching of Charles Darwin's theory of evolution;

> . . . while crimes of passion and organized gang warfare climbed to zenith . . .

America, unaccustomed to her new role—in herself a kind of damned and beautiful Amazon—ignored the warnings of her oracles and the unhappy evidence proliferating in each stratum of the national life.

This was a country poised on a banana peel, but all the Lippmans, Lewises or Menckens in the world could not explain to the ebullient young nor to the ostrich-like old that they were engaged in a marathon dance toward disaster.

Awakening the country from her torpor, under the leadership of such inactivists as Warren Harding and Calvin Coolidge, was to be a slow and torturous process. Yet, the movement had begun.

When the stock market came to its screeching crash in October, 1929, America had almost shed her innocence. She was a part of the rest of the world, although it would take an attack on a naval base at Pearl Harbor before she could understand that adolescence was gone forever and that the responsibility of maturity is not quite the same thing as the pot of gold at the end of a mythological rainbow.

In the meantime, the country asked:

"Ain't We Got Fun?"

CHAPTER ONE

*When
Johnny
Came
Marching
Home*

It was a great day, November 11, 1918—the more so since the bombast of victory had been sounded erroneously four days earlier. The world was waiting for peace. This time it was true.

Somehow, another 155 tons of ticker tape was found to replace all that was used up in the revelry of November 7, and American people, children of innocence, thronged the streets, knowing once and for all that the world was safe for Democracy. After all, hadn't America planned it that way?

At last, after four agonizing years and nearly ten million lives,[1] the Great War was at an end. If there was dancing and jubilation, we had earned it through the blood, sweat and tears which moved us out of our natural isolationism and onto the battlefields of France.

Wilson's Armistice statement was a rational, scholarly invitation to unity. On November 11, that unity was evident in the spirit of celebration. But it was marred from the beginning. A hatred for the "Hun" existed in many hearts, the Kaiser was burned in effigy, and in the souls of some there rankled a desire for punishment and revenge.

Still it was a great day. Three and one-half million American men were still in uniform, two million United States soldiers remained in Europe. Few stopped to think that the casualty lists were not all in, that meatless and wheatless meals were still the law of the land, that the United States was gripped in the throes of a disastrous epidemic of influenza.

Everybody danced. At the Wintergarden, Al Jolson sang the war songs that had thrilled the homefront while the boys were away. Girls reared in a red, white and blue-nosed society surged into the streets to hail the conquering heroes with their kisses. Mothers rushed to their kitchens to produce the best in chicken soup and homemade apple pie.

Doughboys, as the soldiers were called, had lived in trenches, suffered from amoebic dysentery. They had seen bloodshed and horror. They had also met Mlle. de Armentiéres and had learned the pleasures of the grape. They had seen the world from a point of view different from the front porches of midwestern farmhouses, the stoops and fire escapes of Brooklyn. Their ideas of the world had changed forever. But on November 11, 1918, there was reason to rejoice.

If war were Hell, why, then, we were the heroes, martyrs who had died for the sins of our fellows and abolished Hell for all eternity. We, as a nation, had brought about the salvation of the civilized world.

It wasn't quite that simple. Nothing ever is. From the moment of the truce, the seeds of dissatisfaction had begun to sprout. In contrast to the families ecstatic in the joys of reunion, there were those others—whose sons and husbands were lost forever. Gold stars would continue to stud the windows of America for months and years to come. And hadn't Woodrow Wilson pledged himself to keep us out of war? When circumstances had forced him to withdraw that pledge, the country had rallied 'round the flag. But at the end a deep-rooted, suppressed frustration began to flourish.

"It's a long way to Tipperary," but it's a longer way back home. The trail to pre-war ideology, complacency, and ironclad unawareness was overgrown by the thickets of foreign entanglements and pressing, urgent domestic problems.

The Song expressed the country's concern about post-war re-entry problems. Many of the returning doughboys adjusted rapidly. But many others did not. Jobs were few, the world had changed forever.

The world had changed. America had changed. The life-style of the country could not return to a long gone "normalcy." Nothing has ever been the same after *any* war. But we didn't know that then, and so, the hilarity was short-lived.

Production had been feverish during the war. Plants and factories had been called upon to forge the arms and other necessities of combat. Now they were faced with the need to cut back, sharply and at once.

War-induced prosperity was at an end. The day of short hours for high pay was over. It takes time for a war-balanced economy to readjust itself. It would take two years—two years in which increasing numbers of veterans would question a system for which they had fought so valiantly. The country was ill-prepared for their homecoming.

Johnny Doughboy, after his first sight of the American beauty, his first taste of Mom's cooking, his first sense of belonging again, had to address himself to the very real problem of finding employment. Markets were glutted, factories were overstocked. Farmers, who had met the challenge of wartime agricultural production, had overexpanded. Europe, devastated by four years of fighting, could not afford to buy our surplus. Indeed, she could not afford to meet her debts. And what jobs there were in America, the veterans found comfortably filled—often enough by draft evaders and women. Revelations of profiteering from the war which had cost them much filled returning soldiers with revulsion and disgust.

The fear and hatred of Bolshevism, spurred on by Attorney General A. Mitchell Palmer brought out the worst in many Americans. Soldiers who had been taught to hate, to kill, to fight back, broke up the socialist meetings which were already ushering in the Big Red Scare that was to terrify the country in 1919.

Labor, too, took up the cry of violence. If we could teach the Kaiser a thing or two, now we could go to work on well-heeled management. No more high wages? Well and good. Then we will strike, by God. And Wilson! That dewey-eyed idealist . . . he has a lot to learn.

Work stoppages proliferated in the steel mills, coal mines and in the ports stretching the length of the Eastern seaboard. Whole communities were paralyzed.

Suddenly, coming home was not the unalloyed delight it was supposed to have been. The dollar had the purchasing power of $.45, pre-war. Unemployment was rampant. Out of nowhere, the Ku Klux Klan was reassuming a long lost power. The country was staggering under a new debt of $24 billion,[2] and if the girls seemed prettier and the skirts were shorter, it didn't really matter too much in the overall scheme of things.

Some things hadn't changed—not yet. Women did not smoke nor drink (not nice women), talking pictures had not as yet been born, radio was not perfected as a medium of entertainment, sweet sentiment dominated popular music, tea dates took preference over cocktail trysts. But if you wanted a drink you could still buy one in the corner saloon. Prohibition was just around a corner we had yet to turn.

It was a turbulent world, a turbulent country. It could not be put back together again like a jigsaw puzzle that has fallen from its box. Currencies were devalued abroad, trade and traffic routes were forever altered. A decade of swift, convulsive change was beginning.

Sgt. York, about to return to his home state of Tennessee as the most decorated hero of the war, would declare upon his arrival that his faith in God had guaranteed his deliverance. But people were beginning to question the concepts of "glory" and noble "sacrifice" as they would throughout the Twenties as the anti-war writings of Ernest Hemingway, Erich Maria Remarque, and John Dos Passos confirmed in print what many suspected: "Really, in the last analysis, what is the use of all the killing? What is ever gained through the waste of human life?"

Defeated, Germany did not capture what it had envied as "Britain's place in the sun." We did. Caught off guard and unprepared, we didn't know what to do with it, either at home or abroad.

Historian Mark Sullivan suggests that even the old Puritan virtues were experiencing a kind of after-shock. The enforced regimentation of the war years had begun to erode Americans' zeal for self-determination and responsibility. It's always easier to take orders, follow a crowd, than to think for one's self.

It would almost seem that Johnny came marching home to No Man's Land. The Twenties had begun.

[1]Official figures for loss of life, from all war-induced causes were 9,978,771.

[2]The total cost of World War I, as established by the Carnegie Endowment for International Peace, was $337,946,179,657.

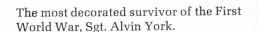

The most decorated survivor of the First World War, Sgt. Alvin York.

CHAPTER TWO

The
Failure
of
a Dream

"My Fellow Countrymen.
The armistice was signed this
morning. Everything for which
America fought has been
accomplished. It will now be
our fortunate duty to assist by
example, by sober, friendly
counsel, and by material aid in
the establishment of just democracy throughout the world."
—Woodrow Wilson,
  November 11, 1918

To the average man on the street the development of jazz, the evolution of the Speakeasy, mattered more than did the Treaty of Versailles. The pain of that debacle would not become evident until the Weimar Republic met its death and the *enfant terrible* of German politics, Adolph Hitler, became a man powerful enough to terrify the world and to slaughter a good portion of it.

Yet no survey of the Twenties could be complete without a discussion of the failure of Woodrow Wilson's dream— a dream that, if fulfilled, might have made the "War to End Wars" a reality and not just a slogan.

We know that things might have been better. But even if Wilson had succeeded there was still a Third World— including all of Africa and Asia—to be dealt with, a fact which occurred to few in the days when the universe seemed comprised of Europe and the United States, and difficult problems were, by today's standards reasonably simple.

Every era needs a tragic hero. Actors, to this day, are prone to tell whomever will listen that a poorly done *Coriolanus* will receive more kudos—and adoring backstage visits— than will a superbly played Iago.

The tragic hero of the postwar years was Woodrow Wilson —dedicated to a better world in a time in which the consensus of his countrymen was: No better world is possible. All we want is steady work, good pay and the grand old U.S.A.

When Woodrow Wilson put forth his 14 points in January, 1918, he had in mind victory without vengeance, peace without reparation. There are those who believe that Wilson was less than sane, there are those who maintain that his ideas reached a pinnacle of naïveté, there are those who believe that if Wilson had been heard—and *heeded* —World War II would not have come about.

Wilson's Grand Idea was that Germany should come out of the war as a nation respected and equal; that out of the quagmire of death and insanity a phoenix should arise— attesting to the brotherhood of man; that an international union—to be called the League of Nations—would foster dignity and truth, virtues which Woodrow Wilson firmly believed would be adhered to by all, once they were demonstrated as a way out of increasing havoc and despair.

His ideals were noble. But after his triumphal arrival in Brest, France, where he was hailed as the savior of the world, our president found himself negotiating at Versailles Palace with three tough-minded gentlemen who were far afield from Wilson in their ideas of how Germany, and the world, should be managed from that day forward.

There they sat: Vittorio Emanuele Orlando, representing Italy, David Lloyd George, representing Great Britain, and Georges Clemenceau, who spoke for France who had lost much to Germany, not only in the Great War but in 1870 as well. These three wanted a declared victory on their own terms, without the face-saving terms Wilson was prepared to give Germany in the light of the Fatherland's resounding defeat. To make a complex situation even thornier, there were those in Washington who considered Wilson's carefully plotted position at Versailles a lot of idealistic nonsense, and they said so.

Fifty years later it is easy to understand why the great powers of Europe wanted Germany in her place, permanently. The country was to rise again to nearly pulverize the continent. Wilson's proposals of freedom of the seas, relaxed trade barriers and a self-respecting Germany were hard to take for the Europeans, although these suggestions had supplied the basis upon which Germany had accepted the 1918 Armistice.

Wilson's dream becomes a nightmare.

The American Congress was overwhelmingly Republican— a fact of life which made Mr. Wilson a less imposing figure at Versailles than he might otherwise have been. He had appealed to his fellow citizens to elect like-minded Democrats only a month before peace was declared. Fed to the teeth with war, and with Wilson, the American public had refused. Further, the president was thoroughly disliked by two prominent Republican partisans, Henry Cabot Lodge of Massachusetts and former president Theodore Roosevelt. They contended that Mr. Wilson did not speak for the great masses of Americans, and the election in November 1918 seemed to bear them out.

Wilson arrived in Europe looking for all the world like a British Prime Minister who had just lost a vote of confidence. The atmosphere was gloomy when the peace conference opened in Paris on January 12, 1919. Negotiations were to continue until the end of June.

Clemenceau, "The Tiger," and Wilson battled bitterly if verbally, throughout the conference. Wilson, whom some considered to be out of his depth when dealing with the elder statesmen of the western world, turned out to be a skilled diplomat, although he tended to deal more with abstractions than with concrete facts.

There were those who considered him a fool. Yet he was to win several victories: French occupation of the Rhineland for only 15 years among them—and a degree of self-determination of nations never before achieved.

On January 25, 1919, Wilson was overjoyed when the Congress agreed to ratify inclusion of the League of Nations in the Treaty of Versailles. Triumph was to be short-lived, however.

Senator Lodge, through a Republican "round robin," signed by 39 senators and senators-elect, spoke out against the League. This less than united home front considerably weakened Wilson's hand in Europe. And thus were sown the seeds of World War II. The covenant, arrived at behind closed doors—in opposition to Wilson's policy of "open covenants openly arrived at" did brand Germany "guilty" for the War. Here at home, some believed the treaty too lenient, others too severe. Almost no one was happy with it.

Roosevelt and Lodge, with the help of their powerful colleagues William Borah of Idaho and Albert Beveridge of Indiana, were to win the day after a series of brilliantly contrived delaying tactics.

Wilson, a believer in taking his message to the people themselves, left Washington on a mission: to sell America on his ideas of a better world and how it could be achieved. This was to be accomplished by a coast-to-coast whistle-stopping tour that would last for months. What little strength the man still had was expended on this trip which was, although soul-lifting at times, basically unsuccessful. Ill, exhausted, the President abruptly returned to Washington from California. Within days he suffered a stroke which paralyzed his left side.

From October, 1919, to March, 1921, America was, in many respects, without a president. Political chaos took charge. The Democratic Party was hopelessly split. Isolationists were at the throats of internationalists. And Wilson was unable, or unwilling, to make concessions to either side. Without their leader, the pro-League forces dissolved before Senator Lodge's powerful coalition. The cause of a generous peace and United States membership in the League was lost.

Bypassing some better candidates—William McAdoo, son-in-law of President Wilson, and Herbert Hoover[1] among them—the feuding Democrats nominated James Cox for the presidency after bitter wrangling during which even the ailing president considered throwing his hat into the political ring for yet a third time. The Republicans, in their wisdom, nominated and elected Warren G. Harding to the White House.

In addition to the disasters of the fight for American membership in the League, the dissension within the ranks of the Democratic Party and the "Big Red Scare" contributed much to the Republican winning of the White House in 1920.

James F. Byrnes, Governor of South Carolina, averred that Bolshevists were plotting an uprising of the southern Negroes. Evangelist Billy Sunday, in an outburst of Christian mercy, called for the death of Socialists and members of the Industrial Workers of the World (Wobblies) before firing squads.

Communist revolts in Hungary and Bavaria caused Americans to think that it could happen here. Little distinction was made between peaceful socialists and actual revolutionaries. Some saw in every radical a wild-eyed bomb thrower, even if the radical were of as gentle a nature as Eugene V. Debs.

In 1919, the Boston police went on strike and there was looting and violence in the streets of that city. Moderates such as Samuel Gompers urged negotiations. And the miners and steel workers were also out on strike. In Seattle, early in 1921, a general strike prevailed. Homemade bombs made their appearances in the homes and offices of public officials across the land. On June 2, 1921, eight bombs exploded in eight cities at the same instant. Obviously, there was a plot going on.

Right—Bolshevism in Russia, and Pro-communist demonstrations in the United States contributed to the Big Red Scare which dominated the political scene in the early years of the decade.

Violence tends to meet hostility. Many persons in sympathy with the striking unions were appalled and sickened by terrorism. J. Edgar Hoover was at the head of an "anti-radical" division in the Justice Department. A. Mitchell Palmer, true to form as the Joe McCarthy of his day, began the raids that were to invade homes and meeting places. Punishment was swift and severe. It was a strange couple of years.

And then it was all over. Sanity began to reappear. There would be further incidents—the bombing of Wall Street's House of Morgan which killed 33 and injured 200, for example. But the intensity of terror had subsided and the bombing, hideous as it was, was viewed as an unfortunate incident rather than as the end of the civilized world.

The man on the street returned to reading the sports and comic pages of his newspaper. Sporadic acts of terrorism were viewed as exactly that: sporadic.

Deportations ceased, calm returned. And on the domestic political scene Wilsonian intensity had vanished. "Normalcy" was the order of the day. But not for everyone. There was the deplorable story of Sacco and Vanzetti—an issue which clouds our reputation as a Democracy to this day.

Peace is rarely with us but, the military-industrial-complex be damned, nearly everyone but Heir Krupp has wanted it. In 1921 the executive secretaries of the Federated Peace Societies of England, Japan and the United States conferred in Washington.

The Ordeal of Sacco and Vanzetti

"They are too bright, we shield our eyes and kill them. We are the dead, and in us there is no feeling nor imagination nor the terrible torment of lust for justice."

—Heywood Broun, referring to the Sacco-Vanzetti case in a 1947 issue of *The New Republic*.

The arrest on May 5, 1920 of Nicola Sacco and Bartolomeo Vanzetti disturbed, at first, a small but articulate minority of American citizens.

Self-confessed anarchists of Italian birth, whose English was not of the best and who had compounded this un-American background with draft evasion during the War, they were arrested on inconclusive evidence for killing two men during a payroll robbery in South Braintree, Massachusetts. The double murder of a paymaster and a guard of a shoe factory proved that the "Great Red Scare" had not as yet abated. In fact, the Monday morning quarterback can clearly see that the bombing by an Italian anarchist of Attorney General Palmer's Washington home on June 2, 1921, sealed the fate of Sacco and Vanzetti before they were ever brought to trial.

"Give me your tired, your poor—"   "America Awakes" to International opinion—too late.

Such exponents of reason as Heywood Broun, Dorothy Parker and Robert Benchley, all highly verbal personalities, spoke out for the two Italians, Broun going so far as to gather testimony that the judge appointed to the case—the Honorable Webster Thayer—was not only anti-radical but considerably less than an Italiophile.

The Judge believed that Vanzetti, at least, was guilty even if innocent, because of his animosity toward "our existing values." Vanzetti, himself, commented "I am suffering because I am a radical and indeed I am a radical; I have suffered because I was an Italian and indeed I am an Italian." And he was right.

The abortion of "justice" which the trial turned out to be, caused one of the greatest polarizations of political ideology in this country since the Civil War. Felix Frankfurter, among others, rose to the defense of the hapless radicals, puncturing the State's case badly. It was to no avail. After testimony from 61 witnesses for the prosecution as opposed to 107 for the defense, the two were sentenced in July, 1921. Demonstrations broke out not only in the Cities of the United States but in Casablanca, France and Uruguay.

It was a case of Establishment versus intellectuals and other social misfits. While Upton Sinclair and Edna St. Vincent Millay joined the liberal camp headed by Broun, the scaremongers would just not quit. Still, as Scott Fitzgerald expressed it, America was uninterested in politics. This was true of many; others were vitally concerned.

Off the bench, Thayer remarked that the two were "anarchist bastards," "Dagos," and " sons of bitches"—hardly a manner of speech expected from a distinguished and presumably unprejudiced jurist. He was prejudiced, of course, finding Sacco and Vanzetti guilty before the evidence was in and communicating his feelings to the jury.

After the conviction, Governor Alvan T. Fuller of Massachusetts appointed a Commission headed by Abbott Lawrence Lowell, then president of Harvard University, to look into the matter. The commission found no reason to reprieve the death sentence, although it did lightly slap the wrist of Judge Thayer for some of his public comments.

And so, at last, Nicola Sacco and Bartolomeo Vanzetti were electrocuted in August of 1927. "With liberty and justice"
—for some.

[1]Among the leaders of the pro-Hoover faction was none other than Franklin Delano Roosevelt, who would in 1932 record a resounding defeat against him.

"The Passion of Sacco and Vanzetti," as realized by crusading painter Ben Shahn.

WOODROW WILSON

"He Kept Us Out of War"
—Democratic Campaign Slogan, 1916

The man who led the United States through the agony of World War I and, through his visionary idealism, sought to ensure a safe and lasting peace for the community of nations (Chapter 5), was the complex product of an unflinching intellectuality, and the prim tenets of Calvinism.

The son of a Presbyterian minister, Woodrow Wilson seemed always to be thinking several generations ahead of his time. The idea of "one world" did not seem so ridiculous when Wendell Wilkie propounded it in the Forties. In the Twenties, it was an unpopular move on Wilson's part to exert presidential pressure to bring about a League of Nations.

Wilson was a man of many talents. He was a prolific writer, excelling in every field he undertook, except fiction. He was an enormously popular teacher who went on to serve as one of the most enlightened presidents in the history of Princeton University.

While there, he introduced the innovative "preceptorial system," designed to create greater rapport between student and instructor. This approach to education is still in use and still respected.

He upgraded Princeton's curriculum. He attempted to banish the ancient and socially-oriented eating clubs—an effort which began to pay off in the 1960s, long after Wilson's death, when students elected to choose membership in more democratic institutions or, frequently, none at all.

In 1910, over a clash concerning the university's graduate school, Wilson felt it necessary to resign his post at Princeton. The New Jersey Democratic organization was delighted, believing that in Wilson it had a gubernatorial candidate who was both respected and naïve. They looked upon him as a ready tool of the machine. He looked at himself as a reform candidate, instrument of the people and of the people only. That's the kind of governor he turned out to be, to the dismay of those who had nominated him.

When he assumed Presidency of the United States in 1913, he knew that the world was in serious trouble, but from the beginning through the end, Woodrow Wilson never wanted war. Fighting contradicted every one of his ideals.

His personal life underwent a tragic change, unexpected on the day of his inauguration. The First Lady, formerly Miss Ellie Lou Axson of Rome, Georgia, died in August, 1914, of Bright's disease compounded by tuberculosis of both kidneys. It was a slow and miserable death.

The man who, although publically dour, had always enjoyed his family—with whom he sang duets and for whom he performed humorous impersonations—found himself alone and bereft. He had been married for 29 years to a wife whom he adored. She was gone. Two of his daughters were married and the third was rarely at home.

The incredible burdens of state weighed heavily on the lonely and conscientious Wilson. He saw the War in Europe growing more deadly, and began to accept the reality that, in time, America was going to have to be a part of it.

At the depth of his personal and professional despair, he met Edith Bolling Galt, chic and outgoing, in every way the opposite of Ellie Axson. But she had a capacity shared by few others in those grim days: she could make the president laugh.

They were married on December 18, 1915, despite rumors engulfing Washington concerning Wilson's relationship with his first wife and another woman, rumors which had basis neither in truth nor in Wilson's Presbyterian character.

The marriage was a happy one, but despite his efforts, Woodrow Wilson was unsuccessful in keeping America out of the war. When he announced his decision to enter the tumult to Congress, in face of some rampant pacifist objections, he heard himself cheered. A kind and deeply troubled man, Wilson commented: "My message for today was a message of death for our young men. How strange it seems to applaud that."

He had tried to save us from war. At war's end, he would try again: to save us with peace.

Following the signing of the armistice, he journeyed to Europe to try to put his League of Nations into effect. He hoped to assure the world, his people, and himself, that all the blood, all the lives had not been sacrificed for nothing.

Europe, which had hailed him at the beginning, wanted peace on different terms. America had lost enthusiasm for her heavily burdened president.

In September 1919, the president, exhausted as he was by the trials of war and the frustrations of peace, set off on a coast-to-coast tour to convince the United States of the rightness of the League.

While traveling, he was stricken with a stroke and endured yet another upon his quiet, almost mysterious, return to Washington.

It has been suggested that the president lived on as a near vegetable, that the First Lady, along with Mr. Wilson's doctor, Cary Crayson, took over the government during his illness. This is not altogether true, although the devoted team did do their best to protect him in his illness. In time, Woodrow Wilson's mind cleared, and sick and broken, he attempted to persuade the Senate into ratification of the Versailles Treaty. He knew what was going on about him to the extent that he considered running for the presidency once again in 1920 in order to complete what he deemed urgent unfinished business He was, of course, not well enough for another term. And even if his health had miraculously returned, the country was through with Mr. Wilson's internationalism. It preferred the presence of Warren G. Harding, and with his election and all that it stood for, began the road through the excessive Twenties and the national tragedies which were to follow.

Woodrow Wilson, who with a strong combination of honesty, perseverance, and reverence for what he believed to be right, died on February 3, 1924 in the small house on S Street, Washington, where he and Edith made their final home. He could die with the knowledge that he had lived his life as well and as fairly as his intelligence, idealism and the changing tenor of his times had allowed.

HEYWOOD BROUN

"Let us hope that one day the frozen Yukon wastes will give him up. Let us hope that something, at least, will give him up. Perhaps he will give himself up. I gave him up long ago."
—Groucho Marx, in an introductory talk about Heywood Broun who was, he said, running for Congress.

Through his column "It Seems to Me," throughout his long years of service on the New York *Tribune* and the New York *World,* Heywood Broun, large and disheveled, was a champion of the underdog and in the forefront of the fight for social justice.

He called them as he saw them, in the ball park, in the courtroom and in the political arena. He was known and respected for his uncompromising honesty which, coupled with his wit, made him an institution.

A born crusader, Broun backed the labor unions and was a founder of the American Newspaper Guild—an enterprise which required ten years of unrelenting work to bring about, in keeping with the anti-union climate of the times.

His writing ranged from collections of his uniformly fine columns to some equally well devised novels.

Married to Barbara Hale, he was father to Heywood Hale Broun, now a prominent sports analyst who possesses the same penchant for words that his father had.

The senior Broun was one of the few to see through the fragile facade of the Jazz Age. He managed to retain his sense of humor along with his devotion to serious causes, but it was this devotion which, at times, got him into trouble. His retirement from the *World* was triggered by his categorical refusal to stop writing about the Sacco-Vanzetti case.

Left of center politically, fascinated by the theatre, Broun was, among other things, a superb sports writer who managed to convey the personalities of the players as well as the drama of the sporting events themselves.

He had a great spirit of fun, and was sometimes dubbed parsimonious by his friends, who teased him about his habit of keeping his poker winnings in a separate pocket so that he would always know how his betting was faring.

Born in Brooklyn in 1888, Harvard-educated as was his compatriot, Robert Benchley, Broun died in 1939, having seen at least some of his aspirations for the common man fulfilled.

MU-RAD MA 20

Turn your switch and get Cuba or Seattle

CHAPTER THREE

In Order to Communicate

The advent of commercial radio changed the face of a nation. Instant communication forged a link between the big cities and the villages and rural areas in between. Intra-national isolationism, of air-born necessity, became a thing of the past.

If the little girl in Idaho now knew what her sister in Manhattan was doing, it was only natural for her to adopt some metropolitan ways.

Radio brought the country together as had no medium of the past. Sharp regional differences would remain, but lack of awareness of the fact and the pace of change would die in all but the most remote farms and hamlets.

November 2, 1920, the date of the Harding-Cox election, marked the opening of KDKA, a Pittsburgh-based station, operated by the Westinghouse Company. At first there were few to receive the station's mostly musical message. But that was to change, radically. Those who heard the election results over radio could probably be numbered in the hundreds. Within five years the increase was to be staggering.

In "The Revolt Against Radio," a piece which appeared in *Fortune* magazine in March, 1947, Dr. Lee De Forest, whose invention of the vacuum tube had helped to get the whole thing going, but whose ideas of what radio should be were decidedly non-commercial, was quoted as saying:

> "What have you gentlemen done with my child. He was conceived as a potent instrumentality for culture, fine music, the uplifting of America's mass intelligence. "You have debased this child, you have sent him out on the streets in rags of ragtime, tatters of jive and boggie-woogie, to collect money from all and sundry for hubba hubba and audio jitterbug. You have made him a laughing-stock to intelligence . . . Soap opera without end or sense floods each household daily . . . Murder mysteries rule the waves by night and children are rendered psychotic by your bedtime stories. This child of mine, now 30 years in age, has been resolutely kept to the average intelligence of 13 years. Its national intelligence is maintained moronic, as though you and your sponsors believe the majority of listeners have only moron minds."

Today's trivia players might be slightly dismayed by Dr. De Forest's assessment of the bases of so many of their games. The radio of the Twenties was a novelty well within the financial reach of many. Whether or not that novelty was an unalloyed boon to the nation or to the world is still hotly debated.

Radio may have produced some intellectual casualties, as Dr. De Forest contended, yet it grew like Topsy. At the Dempsey/Carpentier fight in July, 1921, no fewer than 80 points in the United States were equipped to listen, blow by blow. Within months, radio became a national obsession. Every boy with a modicum of electronic ingenuity was busy building his own receiver, often from a kit. Others were purchasing sets in huge quantity from the Crosley company. Ministers were attempting to save souls through the medium, and music (symphonic as well as "jive") flooded American homes.

Home entertainment, generated from the outside, had been born. Indeed, by 1922 some three million homes possessed radio receivers, status symbols rivaled only by the cars in their garages, the chickens in their pots. By 1925 the great American listening audience was estimated at 50 million.

The dreams of David Sarnoff, who had been trying to convince us all (and, specifically, the Marconi Company) that the world was ready for radio had been realized.

The Sultan of Swat, Babe Ruth, knocked out after running into the right field bleachers in 1924.

Everything flowed from the omnipresent box: music, political commentary, big bands, comedy shows, noise to get up by, noise to go to sleep with (if no better companion could be found), gossip, news, religion. Jazz earned an immediate reputation, developing its ardent fans as well as its detractors, as the soothing saxophone began to take the place of the hitherto ubiquitous violin.

But it was in the world of sports that radio was exceptionally revered. We were a nation of sports addicts, a people more concerned with the outcome of a prize fight than with the course of society and its culture. Radio made it possible to "hear it now" and fans converged around their sets to learn, instantly, how their favorites were doing.

What stars there were!

We have them now—our Joe Namaths, Tommy Agees, Muhammed Alis—and they have their devoted followings. But today hero-worship isn't the single-minded thing it used to be.

In the Twenties, athletic events broke all attendance records. Jack Dempsey, "The Manassa Mauler," brought about the first million-dollar gate. Champions in the various arenas were adored both here and abroad. Sports writers of singular talent emerged: writers such as Ring Lardner, Grantland Rice, Damon Runyon, and Heywood Broun. The result was a continuing love affair between the heroes and the public.

The Twenties boasted Babe Ruth (the Sultan of Swat), Bill Tilden, Bobby Jones, Red Grange, Gertrude Ederle—who swam the English Channel in 1926 at the age of 19—and the still very much alive Jack Dempsey.

Babe Ruth, baseball's star of stars, held the all-time record of doubles, triples and homers—and such was his drawing power that he was eventually lured into the movies (disastrously). In 1927, it was Ruth who scored 60 home runs in 154 games. His lifetime record was 714.

Jack Kelly, father of her Serene Highness Princess Grace of Monaco, won, with Paul Costello, an Olympic rowing contest in Paris.

In golf, the scene was dominated by Robert Tyre Jones, known to all as Bobby, who won his first U.S. Open Championship in 1923. Before the decade was out he would match this feat twice more, along with accumulating assorted amateur and British titles.

Tennis—a sport which attracted women as well as men— claimed as its particular idol "Big Bill" Tilden, who considered himself as much an actor as a tennis player. He was the personification of the grand-stand player, who won his first national singles championship in 1920 and was to go on to win six more.

On the distaff side, Helen Wills had one purpose and one only: to win. She usually did. From 1927 until the end of the Twenties she won every tennis match she entered. Her personality was by no means as engaging as Tilden's, and he is said to have actively disliked her. Miss Wills approached the game as a business or, perhaps, a religion. Mr. Tilden came to the court as though it were a theatre.

For the racing buff, there was Man O' War, considered to be the greatest horse of all time, a huge thoroughbred with an equally large appetite and possessed with compelling speed. In 1919 and 1920, he won 20 out of 21 races. The singular loss was to a horse named, appropriately enough, Upset.

On the football field, there was Red Grange—"The Galloping Ghost"—a quarterback who knew how to carry a ball.

In the ring were Jack Dempsey and Gene Tunney, a pair of properly popular heroes. Their fight at Soldiers' Field, Chicago in 1927, to be known forever as the "Long Count" bout, was broadcast from ringside and it seems as though the whole country was breathless for the outcome. The match proved to be controversial, with Tunney the official winner, although many believed that the laurels should have gone to Dempsey.

Graham McNamee was the commentator at that particular event, as he was at so many others. Those who remember consider him to have been the greatest radio sportscaster of all time.

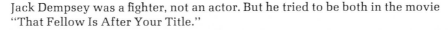

Jack Dempsey was a fighter, not an actor. But he tried to be both in the movie "That Fellow Is After Your Title."

Radio was everyone's source of amusement: the sports fan, music lover, seeker after news as it happened. In the Twenties, despite cinema, Speak-easies, and some truly spectacular theatre, sport was king, and radio brought the superstars into the average American living room, drawing closer the privileged few who actually attended the events and those of us who only dreamed of doing so.

At the end of the decade, 618 stations were in operation, and coast-to-coast broadcasting was a reality, giving voice and fame to such personalities as Rudy Vallee, Jessica Dragonette, the Cliquot Club Eskimos, and Paul Whiteman.

Such expansion was to revolutionize the advertising industry which attempted, with great success, to identify performers with products. While all of this was to appall Dr. De Forest it would, in time, have radio a starmaker comparable only to Florenz Ziegfeld.

The electronic innovation was to change forever the habits of a people who had been able to create their own amusement, only occasionally punctuated by excursions to the Vaudeville palace or the movies. Radio began the trend which television has so vastly expanded: a trend of listening (or watching) rather than *doing*. To tune in was to turn on —or to tune out—depending upon one's point of view.

To the everlasting joy of advertisers everywhere, most people tuned in, absorbed the message of the medium, and then tuned out—just long enough to go out and buy, buy, buy—on credit if need be. This was a time of boom, with radio encouraging big spending every step of the way.

The slogans of the advertisers became part of the speech of almost everyone: "They Satisfy,"[1] "The Pause That Refreshes,"[2] "Reach for a Lucky instead of a Sweet,"[3] "A Skin You Love to Touch."[4] Prior to the Twenties, advertising had largely been confined to prim definitions of a product's virtues. Now it was time for celebrity testimonials, of colorfully printed magazine sales pitches. It is said that Albert Lasker of the Lord and Thomas Agency engineered the first "selling of a president" when he helped to put across the election of Warren G. Harding in 1920.

As Bruce Barton, a founder of the prestigious advertising agency Batten, Barton, Durstine & Osborne, put it: "No important truth can be impressed upon the minds of any large number of people by being said only once."

Radio advertising had a huge, captive audience, and repetition was the name of the game—becoming a part of the slang of the era. How profound were the truths it revealed is a matter of opinion.

[1]Chesterfield Cigarettes; [2]Coca-Cola; [3]Lucky Strike Cigarettes; [4]Woodbury Facial Soap.

HAROLD RED GRANGE

"What a football player—this man Red Grange. He is melody and symphony. He is crashing sound. He is brute force."
—Damon Runyon

All of those weekend widows whose husbands ensconce themselves before the tube for the duration of the professional football season can thank Red Grange for their dilemmas. It was he who made the game respectable.

The "Galloping Ghost" of the University of Illinois, so popular with his fellow students that they wanted him to run for Congress, was a three-time All-American who, in 1924, devastated Michigan with four successive touchdowns of 95, 65, 55 and 45 yards respectively.

It was this great runner who, along with Notre Dame's Knute Rockne, convinced the Eastern sports writers that there was a great, wide world beyond the Ivy League.

Modest almost to a fault, he was a writer's dream. Everything he said or did was good copy. This member of the Football Hall of Fame had averaged five touchdowns a game at high school in Wheaton, Illinois, and was offered scholarships to some 20 colleges. Yet, at Illinois, he hesitated to go out for the team for fear that he might not be good enough.

He was a star and a team player at the same time—a man who invariably shared the credit for a victory with his fellow players. This facet of his personality endeared him to the nation's heart quite as significantly as did his prowess on the field.

Upon graduation, the professional teams were after Grange like a swarm of bees after a honeysuckle bush. His name meant money, and Grange, who said he didn't like football well enough to play for nothing, turned pro—an act that made the sport which, prior to his arrival, had been deemed somewhat declassé—respectable overnight.

He amassed an incredible sum of money playing with the Chicago Bears, New York Giants and the New York Yankees —with whom he earned $1,000 a minute. He was in great demand for testimonials and Arrow Studios paid him $300,000 for his first and only film, *One Minute to Play*, in 1926.

In 1934, age caught up with the legendary quarterback from Illinois, and he retired from the game to pursue a variety of occupations before settling down permanently to a quiet life in Florida.

Unlike so many stars, no matter the arena, Red Grange had invested his fortune wisely while he was earning it, and retirement has been comfortable for the man who was to the gridiron what Babe Ruth was to the baseball diamond. His jersey, tagged with number 77—a number never used again by Illinois—is to this day enshrined at that University in Urbana. In the opinion of most sports writers, that is only fitting. It is unlikely that we shall see such a player again.

WILLIAM HARRISON DEMPSEY

"It was impossible for us to root for Dempsey. He was too methodical and too efficient. It would have been like giving three long cheers for the guillotine as Sydney Carton went to meet it. . . ."
—Heywood Broun after the Dempsey-Carpentier fight.

Born in Manassa, Colorado—a name which would long cling to him, Jack (The Manassa Mauler) Dempsey, former lumberjack and copper miner, made it to the fighting top— fast. In 1918, the 22-year-old heavyweight k.o.'d fighters Fred Fulton and Battling Levinsky. He was ready for a shot at the title. He won it in a fight against defender Jess Willard on July 14, 1919. He retained it for seven years—along with the four million dollars it brought him. Willard was bigger, trained, seasoned. But Dempsey—young, eager, competent— won anyway. The Champ was not able to make it out for Round Four.

In all, the penniless boy had only to defend his title five times, against "Gorgeous Georges" Carpentier in 1921, Elizar Rioux in 1922, Tommy Gibbons and Luis Firpo (the Wild Bull of the Pampas who defeated Dempsey) in 1923, and last, the great Gene Tunney in 1926.

Carpentier was no match for Dempsey, yet the fight brought in more than 90,000 fans and more than a million and a half dollars. The beleaguered Frenchman hadn't a prayer, although Dempsey didn't finish him until the fourth round—in part, perhaps, because the promoters of that Jersey City confrontation didn't want him to. That's showbiz.

All went well with Dempsey, despite some bad press for alleged draft evasion during the war (although he raised $200,000 for the Red Cross) until his 1927 rematch—the "Battle of the Ages—against Gene Tunney. The scene was Soldiers' Field, Chicago, and the gate set a record: $2,658,600. From that famous "long count" fight emerged a new champion. Tunney, making it to his feet on the count of nine, managed to defeat the Champion which had long been his goal as a fighter. If Dempsey had gone immediately to his corner without giving Tunney time to rise, boxing history might well have been different.

Married first to the former Estelle Taylor, Dempsey wasn't much liked by the public or the press, partially because of the wartime activities and particularly because he did not fight Negro contender Harry Wills. Dempsey was not afraid to fight Wills, as many said, but he could not—he averred in later years—find anyone who dared to promote a racially mixed title bout. This was during the resurgence of the Klan, and memories of the triumphs of Jack Johnson, whose tale was recently told in *The Great White Hope*, over white opponents still rankled a good many alabaster souls.

HENRY FORD

*"The way to make automobiles
is to make one automobile like
another automobile, to make
them all alike, to make them
come from the factory just alike
—just like one pin is like
another when it comes from
the pin factory."*
—Henry Ford

Henry Ford, one of the more complex figures in American
industrial history, was born July 30, 1863—in time to grow up
with this country's industrial revolution.

The son of a successful Dearborn, Michigan farmer, Ford
could have lived in quiet comfort if he had chosen to remain
with the family enterprise. But history was forever altered
when the young man realized that farming interested him not
at all and that machines were a source of endless fascination.

At the age of 16, Ford apprenticed himself to a Detroit machine
shop. He knew, even then, that in American industry
machines were more important than human labor, and it was
through this understanding and his meticulous application of
it that Ford was to achieve his outstanding success.

Henry Ford, who was in the flush of triumph to commit some egregious errors in public relations, had the idea that a motorcar could be built, profitably, "for the great multitude." This would be a car within the financial reach of almost everyone, supplying freedom and mobility of an unprecedented kind to the common man. It would also contribute to the increasing sexual looseness that Ford would deplore, but, after all, he was an industrialist, not a sociologist.

In 1909, Henry Ford conceived the Model T—always, inevitably, painted black (the great man had said "to make one automobile like another automobile") and, after its price was drastically reduced in 1914, following the introduction of the moving assembly line, the dream of a car in every garage was on its way to fulfillment.

By the early 1920's, this man who always— and usually successfully—made his own decisions, was producing 60 percent of the nation's automobiles.

Because of his considerable success as a capitalist and his shrewdly humanitarian treatment of his employees—Ford workers received $5 for an eight-hour day in a time in which such payment was unprecedented—Mr. Ford's opinions were solicited on practically everything. For, while his wage and cost profiles were disputed by his colleagues in the automotive industry, the public adored him. That this businessman, who was later to give Franklin Delano Roosevelt all the problems that his fertile brain could muster, was a hero within his own plant is undisputed. Away from the office, he made some historic blunders.

He was an outspoken foe of Judaism, a religion he appears not to have understood, and through his newspaper, the *Dearborn Independent,* he accused that much maligned race of plotting a takeover of the world. Jews were cited as the

cause of all of America's social problems: jazz, short skirts, immorality. Later, when such attacks interfered with Ford's political aspirations, he chose to saddle his devoted publicist, W. J. Cameron, with the fault. He had, he said, no knowledge that such statements were being printed in his paper.

Defeated as Democratic candidate for United States Senator from Michigan, the industrialist responded briefly to a "Ford for President" movement. He was too late. The anti-Semitism of the *Dearborn Independent* had mutilated his campaign and, to some extent, harmed his business.

There were other problems as well. On May 12, 1919, Henry Ford undertook a libel suit against the Chicago *Tribune* for having labeled him in editorials as an "anarchist." The epithet arose from Ford's anti-militarism which had led him to sail to Europe on his legendary "Peace Ship" in an almost singlehanded attempt to bring an end to World War I.

During the trial, incredible gaps in Ford's knowledge of world affairs were revealed. The genius from Dearborn allowed as how "history is bunk" when pressed for certain rudimentary information.

The trial dragged on until, after two million words of testimony, Ford was awarded six cents damages and costs on the ninth jury ballot. If their characters and ideals were not so different, the trial would have been reminiscent of that of scorned playwright, Oscar Wilde. In a sense, Ford had won. But his image had been permanently tarnished.

Henry Ford, a far greater businessman than politician, was reluctant to effect any changes in his Model T, despite the urgings of business associates who recognized, with greater clarity than Ford, the severity of the competition.

When, by the mid-twenties, General Motors had outranked Ford in production and sales, he was at last convinced that the Model T was a thing of the past. The last such car was produced on May 31, 1927.

It required a year and a half to shift gears to go into production of the Model A, which made its appearance on December 2, 1928. Only Henry Ford's grasp of the imagination of the public saved him from ruin. When the car was, at last, unveiled, the man on the street was waiting in line for it. Newspapers were speculating as to what new miracle Mr. Ford had wrought.

Discussion of this monumental occurrence seemed to eclipse conversations of the great trials of the year—Sacco-Vanzetti among them—and tended, at times, to outshout the spectacular crossing of the Atlantic Ocean by Charles A. Lindbergh.

The initial success of the Model A was all that Ford had hoped for. But, within a year, Chevrolet had moved back into the first place it had occupied during Ford's 18-month hiatus.

Ford no longer had it in him to try harder—indeed, he had never ceased to try. For the rest of his years he would have to be content with being number two.

As an old man, he engaged in a certain amount of philanthropy, through the proddings of his wife, the former Clara Bryant. He developed an interest in antiques and Early Americana.

It is difficult to assess the personality of Henry Ford, industrialist and phenomenon. Whatever his motives or his principles, he left his mark on the fabric of a culture.

Consider, for a moment, these statistics: In 1919, there were 6,771,000 personally owned automobiles in this country. In 1929, there were 23,121,000. Now, if you have an hour or two, think upon what these figures have meant for us all.

CHAPTER FOUR

*Of Aberrations,
Nuts
and Miracles*

When the golden mean is abolished and excesses prevail, they can take forms of expression that shock, dismay, cause laughter and effect distraction. A kind of national neurosis can develop. So it was in the Twenties when the world seemed to be plagued with a terminal case of St. Vitus Dance. Fads were rampant.

There wasn't anything so silly about the crossword puzzle, brainchild of Simon and Schuster. It was good clean fun and educational at the same time. It also provided the means to put what has become one of the major publishing houses on the literary map.

There wasn't anything so silly about mah-jongg either, a game imported from China which eclipsed almost every other indoor sport in the 1920s. To be sure, contract bridge had replaced the easier to understand auction bridge, and it had its devotees then as now. But there was something about the clicking of the mah-jongg tiles that made women dress up in best bib and kimono and play the game by rules which differed enormously from coast to coast, from city to city, from expert to expert. The clink of the tiles can still be heard in the ladies' locker rooms of various American country clubs, and similar sounds emanate from nearly every store front in the Hong Kong of the Seventies. As an all-enthralling American pastime, it went the way that canasta was eventually to follow, while bridge, less heralded at the time, has endured and even increased its following. Mah-jongg was pleasant, it was harmless.

There was plenty that was silly about the Miss America contest, conceived to extend the Atlantic City "season" for a week after Labor Day and which, like some rehashed melody, continues to linger on. It was exhausting for the contestants, but it was innocent enough—despite the outrage of certain bluenoses at the amount of pulchritudinous flesh there displayed. Yet who could blame the young ladies for entering the arena? There is something compelling about the Cinderella complex, the nobody becoming somebody over night. From its inception in 1920, that has been the special lure of the Miss America business.

The early entries weren't the talented college girls who tend to flock to Atlantic City like so many lemmings every year in a more serious-minded age. They were average—to the point of homeliness in many instances. And Bert Parks wasn't around to project his ebullience into the goings-on. But it was good for the promoters, it was good for Atlantic City and, well, girls will be girls and boys will always be on hand to look at them. Suffrage notwithstanding, the contestants were there for the ogling, and the "pageantry" of Miss America was on its vainglorious way. Anyone who did not approve simply did not need to attend.

Far more serious was the advent of marathon dancing,
a craze which took its toll on the health of American youth.
It was the endurance contest to end endurance contests, and
for some perverse reason we liked to stand around and
watch these people dance for days and nights on end until
they dropped from sheer exhaustion or, frequently, from
fatal heart attacks. One enterprising young dancer soaked
her feet in brine to keep them immune from pain during these
man-killing assaults on the intelligence (and physical
stamina). Most of the rest were content to stop for 15
minutes after each hour of dancing and, looking for all the
world like tormented fugitives from lunatic asylums, allow
their feet a few minutes of rest and massage.

There was money to be made for the successful participant,
but the spectacle was so ludicrous as to make goldfish
swallowing seem like a solemn avowal of sanity and
bull-fighting appear to be a paramount display of humanity.
After all, marathon dances gave steady employment to
nurses and doctors, who might otherwise have been
relegated to the treatment of the poor and the sick.

Cheek to Cheek, jowl to jowl, or belly to belly, marathon dancing endured
longer than many of the dancers. This photograph was made at the end of
3,327 hours of dancing. The ludicrous had reached an apex.

Maybe because we had learned to think of ourselves as a hardy people in pioneer days, endurance was so pleasing to the man on the street that it was flaunted through other means than the dance floor. There were endurance races by automobile, for example, and there was the most pointless waste of time of all: that of "sitting on top of the world." In this instance, the world was a flagpole. It began with a man named Shipwreck Kelly who, in 1924, took up his unlikely career in Hollywood. Sitting up there in the sky, his task was to lure patrons into a theatre, and it worked so well that by 1929, Kelly had lived out a full 145 days and nights perched precariously atop the flagpoles of the country.

He even met his wife from this curious vantage point— an 18-year-old girl who slapped the face of one of Shipweck's more serious scoffers. When he at last descended from his aerie, the two were married—a union which was to endure for six years until the young wife came to believe that her charms were not competition enough for the flagpole where her husband spent so much of his time and thus sued for divorce.

Kelly and his emulators subsisted on liquid diets which were hoisted up to them at periodic intervals. A serious question as to the availability of plumbing devices arises—one would suppose that the "sitters" were human—but research offers no clues as to how that particular problem was managed in flagpole feats which sometimes lasted for as many as ten days.

URSULA: "Is my nose shiny, Dearie?"
LAMBERT: "No, but your right knee is dusty."

Right—Nonsense was the name of the game, and Shipwreck Kelly (world famous flagpole sitter) was the personification of nonsense. The fad caught on and Shipwreck "performed" from Los Angeles to Broadway.

"X MARKS the SPOT"
BROADWAY THEATRE
53rd St. at Broadway
NOW PLAYING

WHEN
SHIPWRECK KELLY
SURVIVES
He'll go to...
ROTH
MOTOR CARS
1700 B'WAY
for a
USED CAR
Why not you?

This phenomenon attracted the young of both sexes and was singularly popular in Baltimore, Maryland, a town that could be home to H. L. Mencken and some 20 "sitters," all of whom were functioning in their rather macabre fashion at the same time, to the great delight of Baltimore's mayor who hailed the "achievement."

Even religion was not immune to the prevalent hysteria. The evangelists were at a peak of fervor they had not attained before and have yet to attain again. Along with the fabulous and famous Aimee Semple McPherson and Billy Sunday (the man who could not shut down Chicago) were the small town preachers, paid considerably less, who were available to lead revival meetings that offered Main Street opportunity to let off some of the emotional steam that rapidly changing times were creating.

Perhaps the increase in the old-fashioned, hymn-shouting approach to God had come about in reaction to the revolt of the intellectuals from the religious values of their parents. But it became clear during the Twenties that the feelings of the Deep South about the celebrated Monkey Trial (Chapter 5) were not isolated in that region alone. "If it was good enough for Grandpa, then it's good enough for me," or so sang the small town pious.

It was Billy Sunday himself who proclaimed over the "body" of John Barleycorn (who represented all of the evils of drink) that, through Prohibition, "the reign of tears is over." It wasn't, but one can almost hear a chorus of "Amen, Brother" as Sunday presided at the pseudo-funeral.

The forces of reaction weren't limited to the churches alone. The resurgent Ku Klux Klan came 40,000 strong to March on Washington in 1925. Clearly, it was madness, madness everywhere and never time to think.

On college campuses, it was fashionable to study little, party much, and to dip into fountains, dance on table tops and in every conceivable sort of way emulate the antics of Scott and Zelda Fitzgerald, the hero and heroine of pleasure-seeking youth. It wasn't so much Scott's genius that attracted the younger generation whom he had analyzed so vividly in his work. It was his life-style that got to them. That they copied; his writing they did not.

Sex was a favorite topic, sex-appeal or "it," as personified by Clara Bow, was the prime virtue to possess. Powdered knees, thin dresses, center-parted hair, all were sex symbols. It seemed that after years of repression everyone was obsessed with sex.

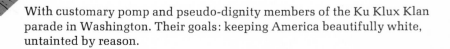

With customary pomp and pseudo-dignity members of the Ku Klux Klan parade in Washington. Their goals: keeping America beautifully white, untainted by reason.

Chicago would not
yield to Billy Sunday,
but much of the nation would.

White sheeted Klansmen descend
upon Richmond, Virginia in 1920.
The night riders had deserted
their horses for the increasingly
popular automobile.

The average college Joe thought he looked like Rudolph Valentino, and his "Sheba" spoke a language all her own. While outwardly disdainful of established conventions, everyone attended the football games, wanted to "go Greek" (join a sorority or fraternity), flipped over the captain of the football team who, despite the oft-sounded new values of the day, continued to claim his place in the collegiate hierarchy over the chairman of the debating team.

Nobody seemed to know where he was going or why— and the few who had any idea escaped to the Bohemias here and abroad (Chapter 8). For the rest, it was hijinks and gin all the way—and to hell with everything else.

Hollywood, ever in the fore when it came to nonsense, enlivened the pages of the tabloids with the case of Fatty Arbuckle and Virginia Rappe.

ARBUCKLE TAKES THE RAPPE

Roscoe (Fatty) Arbuckle, whose life's work had ostensibly been devoted to enriching the happiness of the nation's children, came to an ignoble end—whether through excessive obesity or a perverted sexual disposition it is hard to say.

It happened in San Francisco, at the still elegant St. Francis Hotel. And what happened was too much even for Hollywood, surfeited as it was with sex and sensationalism on the silver screen.

Virginia Rappe, 23, left a drinking party with Arbuckle on September 5, 1921. The pretty model and actress was to linger for four days after the encounter. With her death would come the demise of Arbuckle's career.

This much is known:

The lovely Miss Rappe died of a ruptured bladder, complicated by peritonitis, following sexual relations with Arbuckle. The State of California attributed the cause of death to "external pressure" on the bladder—and there can be no question but that Fatty could exert a lot of pressure.

There were other possible causes, many of which surfaced during the three trials which brought scandal to Hollywood and permanently wrecked Fatty's reputation. One school held that, upon hearing Miss Rappe's screams of distress, friends who believed that she had drunk too much promptly submerged the ill-starred starlet in a tub of cold water. Doctors were on hand at the trial to testify that the cold could have ruptured the bladder. Arbuckle, all 320 pounds of him, asserted that the rupture had been caused by a bladder already damaged by consumption of too much alcohol of inferior quality. There can be no doubt that Miss Rappe's clothing and boudoir were in a state of disarray when Arbuckle left her. There is considerable doubt as to why and how. The ensuing trials for manslaughter resulted in two hung juries and an eventual acquittal for the jovial comedian.

But the days of wine and roses were over. Blacklisted by every studio, Arbuckle did some minor directing and, in 1933, was featured by Warner Brothers in a few low budget two-reelers. On the final day of shooting of the last of them, the one-time star, elated by his re-emergence on the national scene, went to bed a happy man. That night he died in his sleep at the age of 46.

Fatty Arbuckle, innocent of innocents (until later) makes time with a mock up bride.

Sincerely
Rudolph Valentino

The death of the world's greatest lover, Rudolph Valentino, went on to produce the most garish and tasteless funeral of a garish and tasteless era. Although the service itself was held in New York City, it was Hollywood all the way. In an open casket, the man who immortalized the Sheik, lay in full view of 30,000 weeping fans who came for a last view of his magnificent person—each fan allowed about one second to bestow her sorrowful gaze.

On the day of the funeral itself, 100,000 of the young actor's mourners gathered in the rain to pay him final respect. In their grief, some women were known to have killed themselves, many others fainted. Still others were trampled in the rush for a final glimpse of the great man.

Many feminine eyes were misty upon the death of actor Rudolph Valentino, but there were those nearly prostrate in their grief. Some admirers knelt in prayer beside his bier.

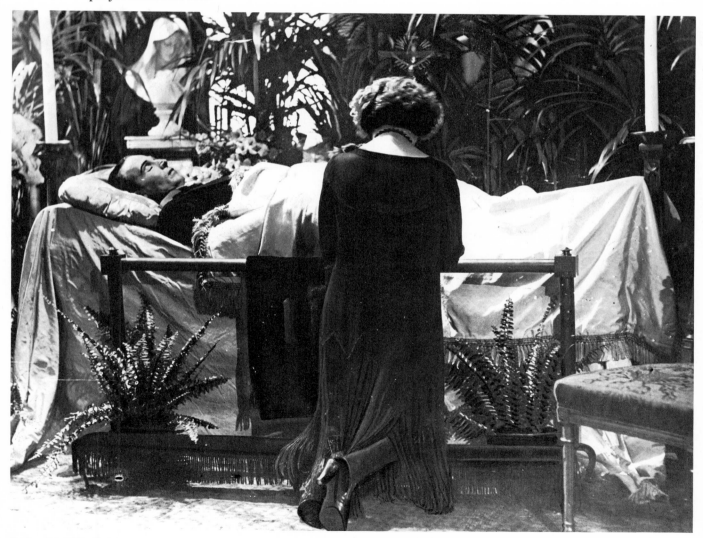

Left—The Sheik.

Sometimes, of course, even the Twenties stopped long enough to take note of something that really mattered: the history-making flight of Charles A. Lindbergh among them. Once again, there was hysteria in the streets but this time there was good reason for it. Here was a genuine miracle.

Lindbergh's achievement not only established him as what the Japanese call a "Living National Treasure," but it also did much to vindicate Brigadier General Billy Mitchell, a World War I aviator who had sought to establish an Air Force independent of the U. S. Army. He was considered something of a rebel, and few in power took him seriously, nor did they actually entertain the idea that air would be the means of transportation (and warfare) of the future. He was court-martialed for his views and for his efforts to put his point across. Now, with Lindbergh's triumph, Billy Mitchell didn't seem as out of touch with reality as he had before.

Everyone had to find an outlet for his hysteria, which is, perhaps, why some of the trials—solemn or just plain ugly— of the decade received the inordinate followings that they did. There wasn't a Charles Manson, but there was a Leopold and a Loeb. To learn of them, and their crimes, read on.

Charles Lindergh conquered the Atlantic and the imagination of his countrymen. Upon his return from Paris, New York City turned out to greet the nation's hero.

LAST WILL AND TESTAMENT OF RUDOLPH GUGLIELMI.

- - - O - - -

IN THE NAME OF GOD, AMEN: I, RUDOLPH GUGLIELMI, of the city of Los Angeles, County of Los Angeles, State of California, being of sound and disposing mind and memory and not acting under the duress, fraud or undue influence of any person or persons whatsoever, do hereby make and publish this my LAST WILL AND TESTAMENT in the manner following, that is to say:

FIRST: I hereby revoke all former Wills by me made and I hereby nominate and appoint S. George Ullman of the city of Los Angeles, County of Los Angeles, State of California, the executor of this my LAST WILL AND TESTAMENT, without bonds, either upon qualifying or in any stage of the settlement of my said estate.

SECOND: I direct that my Executor pay all of my just debts and funeral expenses, as soon as may be practicable after my death.

THIRD : I give, devise and bequeath unto my wife, Natacha Rambova, also known as Natacha Guglielmi, the sum of One Dollar ($1.00), it being my intention, desire and will that she receive this sum and no more.

FOURTH: All the residue and remainder of my estate, both real and personal, I give, devise and bequeath unto S. George Ullman, of the city of Los Angeles, County of Los Angeles, State of California, to have and to hold the same in trust and for the use of Alberto Guglielmi, Maria Guglielmi and Teresa Werner, the purposes of the aforesaid trust are as follows: to hold, manage, and control the said trust property and estate: to keep the same invested and productive as far as possible: to receive the rents and profits therefrom, and to pay over the net income derived therefrom to the said Alberto Guglielmi, Maria Guglielmi and Teresa Werner, as I have this day instructed him; to finally distribute the said trust estate according to my wish and will, as I have this day instructed him.

-1-

RUDOLPH VALENTINO

"Catnip to women"
—H. L. Mencken

Valentino, the immortal "Sheik" of the silent screen, set women on their ears and caused young men to copy his hair style, his tango and his facial expressions—as best they could.

His life was short—he died in 1926 at 31—and his career spanned but five years. But what a career it was!

Rodolpho Alfonzo Raffaeli Pierre Filibert di Valentina d'Antonquolla, the man who was to electrify the world was born to an Italian father and French mother. He left his native Italy in 1913 to seek his fortune in America. Fortune didn't come immediately. Valentino worked as a gardener and as a bus boy before he was spotted dancing. After that he was tested for his first movie and with the release of *The Four Horsemen of the Apocalypse* he was never to be out of work. He was honored for his performance as Armand in *Camille* and, of course, for his portrayal of the hot-blooded *Sheik*. Women adored him, but men tended to be indifferent.

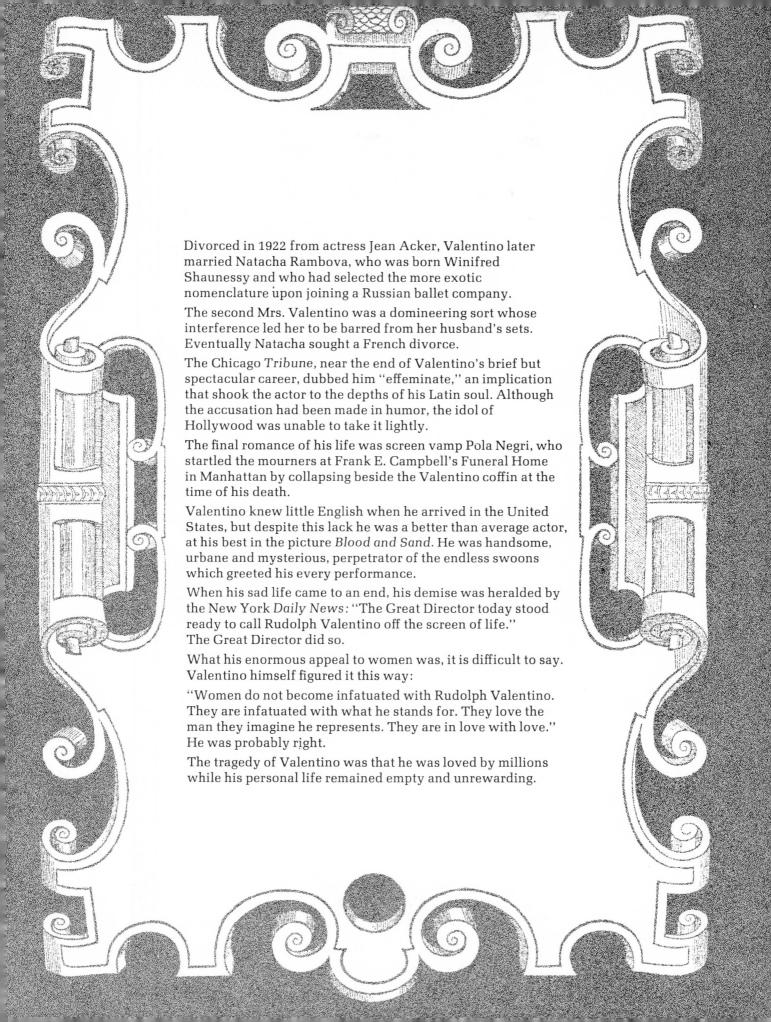

Divorced in 1922 from actress Jean Acker, Valentino later married Natacha Rambova, who was born Winifred Shaunessy and who had selected the more exotic nomenclature upon joining a Russian ballet company.

The second Mrs. Valentino was a domineering sort whose interference led her to be barred from her husband's sets. Eventually Natacha sought a French divorce.

The Chicago *Tribune,* near the end of Valentino's brief but spectacular career, dubbed him "effeminate," an implication that shook the actor to the depths of his Latin soul. Although the accusation had been made in humor, the idol of Hollywood was unable to take it lightly.

The final romance of his life was screen vamp Pola Negri, who startled the mourners at Frank E. Campbell's Funeral Home in Manhattan by collapsing beside the Valentino coffin at the time of his death.

Valentino knew little English when he arrived in the United States, but despite this lack he was a better than average actor, at his best in the picture *Blood and Sand.* He was handsome, urbane and mysterious, perpetrator of the endless swoons which greeted his every performance.

When his sad life came to an end, his demise was heralded by the New York *Daily News:* "The Great Director today stood ready to call Rudolph Valentino off the screen of life." The Great Director did so.

What his enormous appeal to women was, it is difficult to say. Valentino himself figured it this way:

"Women do not become infatuated with Rudolph Valentino. They are infatuated with what he stands for. They love the man they imagine he represents. They are in love with love." He was probably right.

The tragedy of Valentino was that he was loved by millions while his personal life remained empty and unrewarding.

CHARLES A. LINDBERGH JR.

"Science, freedom, beauty, adventure: what more could you ask of life? Aviation combined all the elements I loved ... In flying I tasted the wine of the gods ..."
—Charles Lindbergh in 1953

If, in those early days of aviation in which Charles A. Lindbergh captured the international imagination to become a worldwide celebrity, there were those who wished to rain on his parade, it seems, from this distance, fairly certain that Lindbergh was unaware of it. In fact, he seems curiously detached from all of the kudos and displays of recognition which sprung up around him.

He was the hero's hero at a time when a hero was acclaimed and worshiped by nearly everyone.

Two years before he enchanted the world by completing the first solo flight to Paris from New York, Lindbergh had already begun to make his aviational mark.

In 1925, while participating in maneuvers over Kelly Field in Texas, the then Cadet Lindbergh collided with the plane of another student pilot and was forced to bail out. This act of survival won him admission to the exclusive "Caterpillar Club," made up of aviators who had endured similar ordeals. He was to bail out three more times before the accomplishment which shook and shrunk the world.

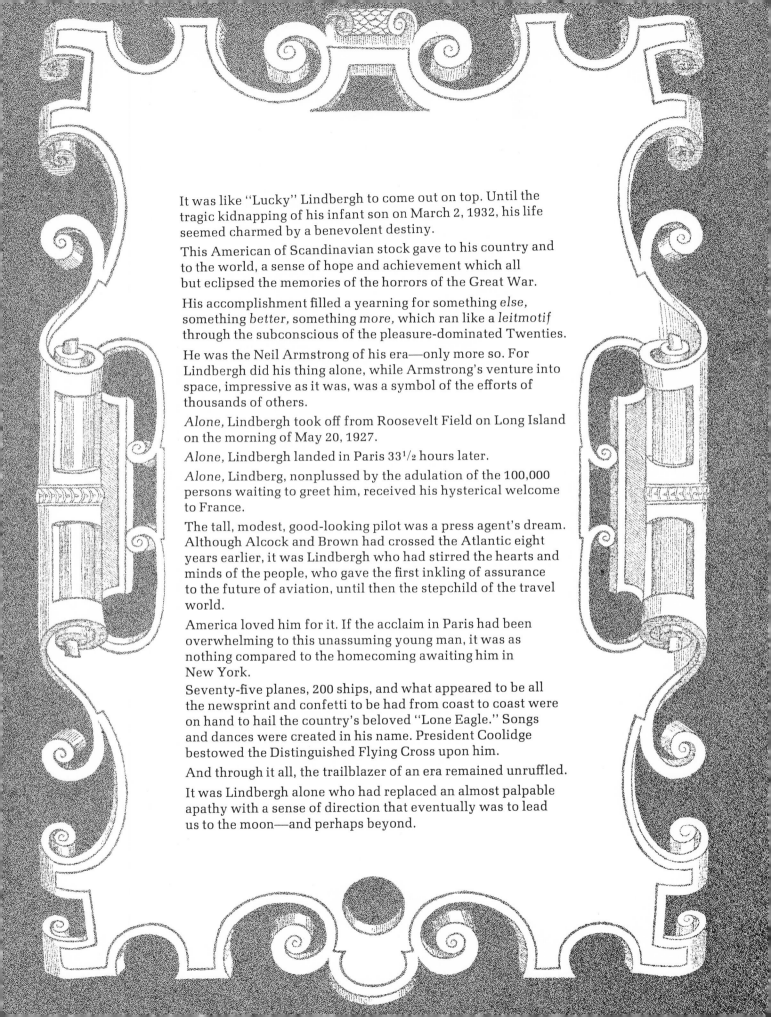

It was like "Lucky" Lindbergh to come out on top. Until the tragic kidnapping of his infant son on March 2, 1932, his life seemed charmed by a benevolent destiny.

This American of Scandinavian stock gave to his country and to the world, a sense of hope and achievement which all but eclipsed the memories of the horrors of the Great War.

His accomplishment filled a yearning for something *else*, something *better*, something *more*, which ran like a *leitmotif* through the subconscious of the pleasure-dominated Twenties.

He was the Neil Armstrong of his era—only more so. For Lindbergh did his thing alone, while Armstrong's venture into space, impressive as it was, was a symbol of the efforts of thousands of others.

Alone, Lindbergh took off from Roosevelt Field on Long Island on the morning of May 20, 1927.

Alone, Lindbergh landed in Paris 33½ hours later.

Alone, Lindberg, nonplussed by the adulation of the 100,000 persons waiting to greet him, received his hysterical welcome to France.

The tall, modest, good-looking pilot was a press agent's dream. Although Alcock and Brown had crossed the Atlantic eight years earlier, it was Lindbergh who had stirred the hearts and minds of the people, who gave the first inkling of assurance to the future of aviation, until then the stepchild of the travel world.

America loved him for it. If the acclaim in Paris had been overwhelming to this unassuming young man, it was as nothing compared to the homecoming awaiting him in New York.

Seventy-five planes, 200 ships, and what appeared to be all the newsprint and confetti to be had from coast to coast were on hand to hail the country's beloved "Lone Eagle." Songs and dances were created in his name. President Coolidge bestowed the Distinguished Flying Cross upon him.

And through it all, the trailblazer of an era remained unruffled.

It was Lindbergh alone who had replaced an almost palpable apathy with a sense of direction that eventually was to lead us to the moon—and perhaps beyond.

CLARA BOW

"You either have it or you don't"
—Elinor Glyn

Clara Bow, the "IT" (Sex Appeal) girl of the gin-soaked Jazz Age, was a genuine Cinderella, but her fairy tale turned out to have an unhappy ending. Born in 1905 to poverty-stricken Brooklyn parents, she grew up feeling rejected, unloved, unwanted. She was never to dispel these emotions.

Her father, a carpenter, tried to make straggling ends meet, but he was largely unsuccessful. Her mother had not been well since the births and deaths of the two babies who preceded Clara. It was a gloomy atmosphere and the future sex symbol of a decade determined at an early age to get out.

In 1922, the red-haired, well-rounded beauty entered a contest searching for "The Most Beautiful Girl in the World." She won, and she was on her way, although her deranged mother was so appalled that she attempted to stab the fledgling starlet.

Miss Bow's first few pictures were insignificant and netted her little, but eventually she was hired by Paramount. In 1926, she became known as the personification of flaming youth, and her success in films was assured.

She soon accumulated all of the paraphernalia of stardom including red chow dogs and a large red car to match her hair. She dated men of such spectacular prominence as actor Gary Cooper and director Victor Fleming.

She liked parties, crowds, and gaiety—but her sense of loneliness and rejection was not to leave her, not even at the dazzling heights of her career.

Eventually the Talkies (Clara had an unfortunate and harsh Brooklyn accent) and some nasty little scandals finished her reign in Hollywood. By 1931, Paramount chose to terminate her contract—although the rupture was said to have come about through "mutual consent."

Still searching, she married cowboy actor Rex Bell and twice tried to stage a comeback. Apparently, defeat was in her horoscope. A series of breakdowns followed and Clara Bow had made that short but tragic trip from the top of the heap to a sanitarium.

It was the end for one of the top five Hollywood box office attractions, who had had a unique quality for driving men into frenzy. She had bathed in perfume, adored fast cars and high living. She had endured a frenetic existence and she had learned that she could not enjoy the pace which she had set for herself.

There is irony here: fighting to escape poverty, misery and loneliness, achieving wealth and acclaim while the misery and loneliness remained unabated, Clara Bow found the world too much for her—both in the sandlots of Brooklyn and on the back lots of Hollywood.

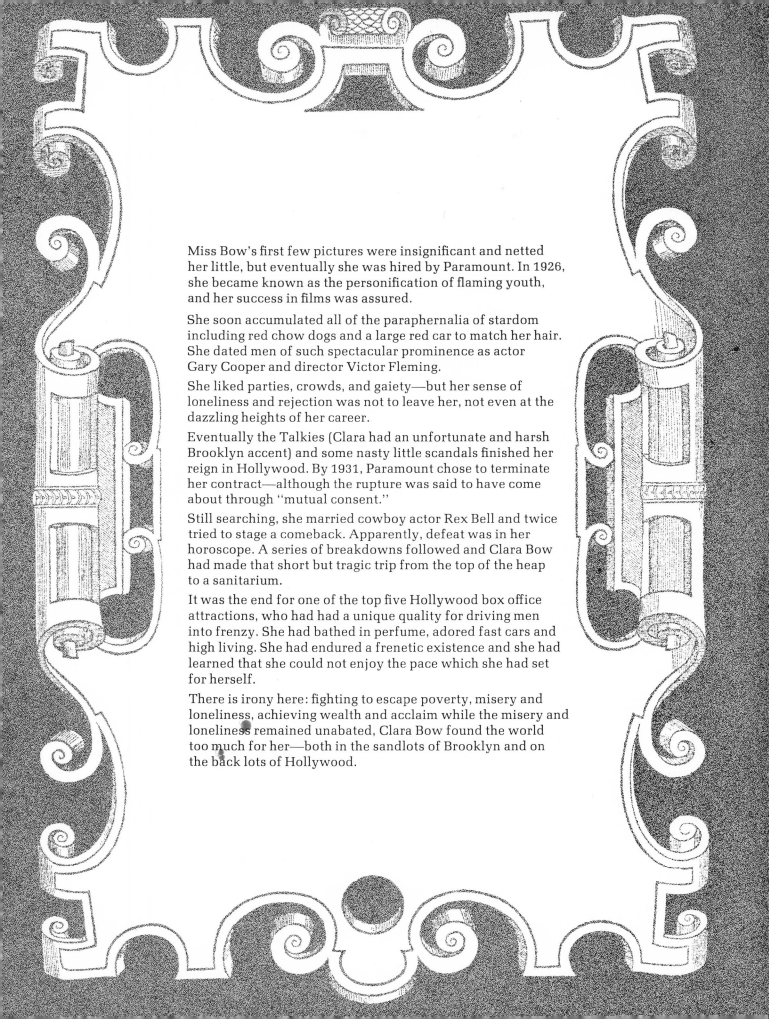

AIMEE SEMPLE McPHERSON

*"Our civilization is still in a
middle stage, scarcely beast, in
that it is no longer wholly
guided by instinct; scarcely
human, in that it is not yet
wholly guided by reason."*
—Theodore Dreiser in
Sister Carrie

"I am not a healer," the woman often proclaimed, preferring as she said, to give the credit to the Lord.

But if Aimee Semple McPherson were indeed bereft of healing powers, she was nevertheless the embodiment of the marriage of show business and religion. Evangelism flourished; Billy Sunday threatened to shut down Chicago; the ravages of Hell's fire were announced from a thousand pulpits. Aimee was the undisputed Queen of evangelism. She knew the value of timing, lighting, settings and music. Most important, she knew and stressed the value of fun.

From homebase, Angelus Temple in Los Angeles, the once-widowed, eventually twice-divorced, Sister Aimee spread her message of joy: the "Foursquare Gospel" based upon the delights of heaven's glorious reward.

The formula worked. Canadian born, Mrs. McPherson began her career in China as the 17-year-old bride of Robert Semple, a missionary. Left a widow, shortly before the birth of her first child, she returned to the United States, in time married Harold McPherson, and appeared to settle down to

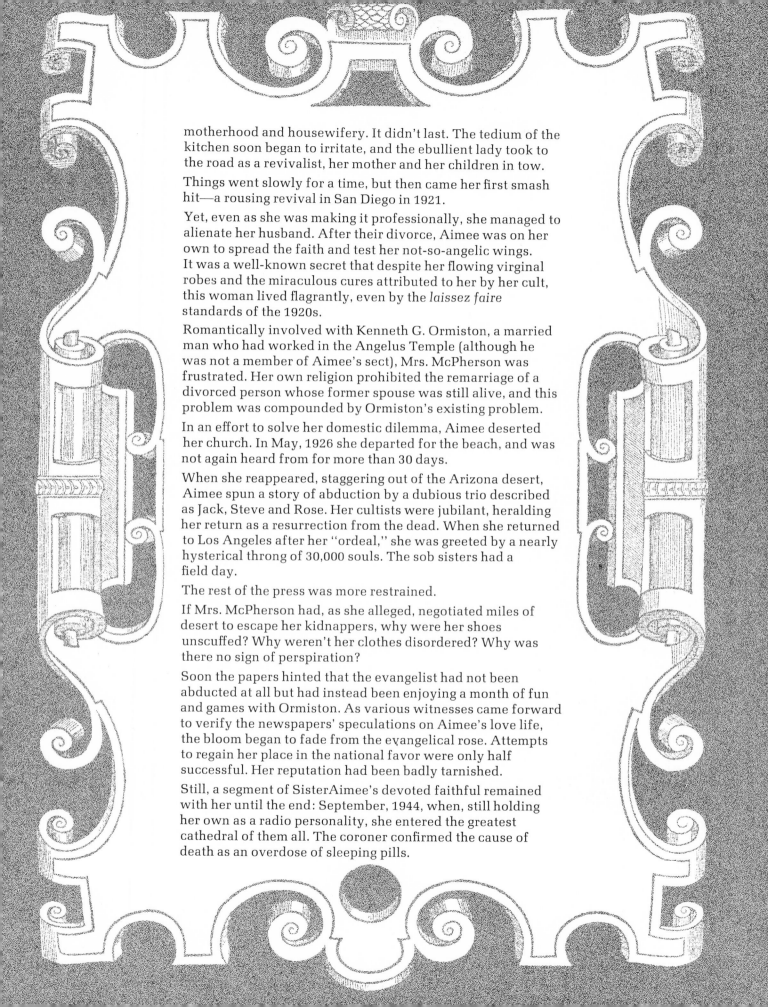

motherhood and housewifery. It didn't last. The tedium of the kitchen soon began to irritate, and the ebullient lady took to the road as a revivalist, her mother and her children in tow.

Things went slowly for a time, but then came her first smash hit—a rousing revival in San Diego in 1921.

Yet, even as she was making it professionally, she managed to alienate her husband. After their divorce, Aimee was on her own to spread the faith and test her not-so-angelic wings. It was a well-known secret that despite her flowing virginal robes and the miraculous cures attributed to her by her cult, this woman lived flagrantly, even by the *laissez faire* standards of the 1920s.

Romantically involved with Kenneth G. Ormiston, a married man who had worked in the Angelus Temple (although he was not a member of Aimee's sect), Mrs. McPherson was frustrated. Her own religion prohibited the remarriage of a divorced person whose former spouse was still alive, and this problem was compounded by Ormiston's existing problem.

In an effort to solve her domestic dilemma, Aimee deserted her church. In May, 1926 she departed for the beach, and was not again heard from for more than 30 days.

When she reappeared, staggering out of the Arizona desert, Aimee spun a story of abduction by a dubious trio described as Jack, Steve and Rose. Her cultists were jubilant, heralding her return as a resurrection from the dead. When she returned to Los Angeles after her "ordeal," she was greeted by a nearly hysterical throng of 30,000 souls. The sob sisters had a field day.

The rest of the press was more restrained.

If Mrs. McPherson had, as she alleged, negotiated miles of desert to escape her kidnappers, why were her shoes unscuffed? Why weren't her clothes disordered? Why was there no sign of perspiration?

Soon the papers hinted that the evangelist had not been abducted at all but had instead been enjoying a month of fun and games with Ormiston. As various witnesses came forward to verify the newspapers' speculations on Aimee's love life, the bloom began to fade from the evangelical rose. Attempts to regain her place in the national favor were only half successful. Her reputation had been badly tarnished.

Still, a segment of SisterAimee's devoted faithful remained with her until the end: September, 1944, when, still holding her own as a radio personality, she entered the greatest cathedral of them all. The coroner confirmed the cause of death as an overdose of sleeping pills.

CHAPTER 5 Some Incredible Trials

The stories which made headlines during the 1920s pointed up the tastes of a culture gone mad. A vivid example of what happens to people when they run out of values was the murder of young Bobby Franks, 13-year-old son of a Chicago millionaire, by Richard (Dickie) Loeb and Nathan (Babe) Leopold.

There was no motive behind the macabre action of these wealthy University of Chicago graduate students except, perhaps, a perverted drive for kicks and a desire to perpetrate the perfect crime. In short, it was murder for the fun of it all. The choice of Bobby Franks as victim was, as the radio used to say, purely coincidental. He was simply there, available, walking home from the exclusive Harvard School for Boys, when he accepted a ride from Leopold (19) and Loeb (18).

The date was May 21, 1924—a year in which violation of the law, in part at least a reaction to Prohibition, was commonplace. But murder, accepted rather calmly by the public when it happened to gangsters, was not commonplace when it came to an innocent child. Even the cynicism of the Twenties could not permit a sanguine view of this sort of outrage.

Bobby Franks did not hesitate to climb into the death car. He admired his murderers, who had achieved certain acclaim in the Hyde Park section of Chicago for their intellectual feats. Bobby Franks had no reason to suspect that within a few blocks of his comfortable home he would be gagged, his skull shattered by a heavy chisel, his face drenched in hydrochloric acid to prevent ready identification, his body deposited in a culvert bordering the Pennsylvania railroad near the outskirts of the city. Later, Nathan Leopold was to refer to Bobby as "a nice little boy." It had not occurred to Bobby that he would be treated as anything else.

What Leopold and Loeb lacked in humanity, they made up for in aplomb. While the Franks family grew uneasy, then frantic, at Bobby's failure to return from school—for this was some 40 years before the run-away child syndrome had become an everyday occurrence—the two prodigies drank liquor and played cards. If they felt any contrition over their monstrous act, they concealed it from the world and, it seems, themselves.

At 10 p.m. the Frankses' telephone rang—several hours after the murder. A man who identified himself as "Johnson" told Mrs. Franks that the missing boy would be returned unharmed if certain instructions were faithfully carried out. After four agonizing hours, Jacob Franks, the boy's father, reported the disappearance and the telephone call to the police. He urged, from fear for his boy's life, that the case be kept secret.

On May 22, the day following the murder, the Franks received a second communication from their son's alleged kidnapper. At 9 a.m. a special delivery letter arrived, typed and signed in type by the mysterious George Johnson. It demanded $10,000 in small, used bills, to be deposited in a cigar box and left at an assigned place. At 1 p.m. Mr. Franks received instructions for delivery of the currency and set out to place it exactly where he had been told.

In an ironic twist of fate, Bobby Franks' nude body, battered and acid-scarred, was discovered while his father was away from home in a desperate fool's errand to save the son he believed to be still alive.

The clues were minimal, but they were enough. A pair of thick-lensed eyeglasses were found with the body (Bobby Franks did not wear spectacles)—glasses which would eventually be traced to Leopold. The type of the ransom note compared exactly with the print of Leopold's Underwood— a machine which had been hidden but was readily located.

When the two boys, both scions of wealthy and well-respected Jewish families, were arrested for murder, the shock waves emanating from Chicago reverberated across the country.

Clarence Darrow, humanitarian's humanitarian, pleads for the lives of Richard Loeb and Nathan Leopold during their trial for the murder of 13-year-old Bobby Franks. Darrow succeeded. At left foreground sits Jay Kerr, prominent songwriter.

Brilliant attorney Clarence Darrow, then 68 years old, was called in to defend the two murderers. While he had few, if any, doubts as to their guilt, he also abhorred capital punishment. He was not in court to free Nathan Leopold and Richard Loeb but, rather, to save them from execution.

Darrow chose not to defend the boys on the basis of insanity —narrowly defined as the inability to distinguish right from wrong. Instead, he used the term "mental illness," turning to his knowledge of Freudian psychology to describe Leopold as a manic paranoiac and Loeb as a schizophrenic. Drawing upon his own powers as an orator and vast intellectual awareness, Darrow managed to talk for two days about the emotional immaturity of the boys, as opposed to their supernormal intellects.

There was no jury. On September 10, 1924, moved by Darrow's eloquence and logic, Judge John R. Caverly, Chief Justice of Cook County's Criminal Court, sentenced each of the young, thrill-seeking geniuses to life-imprisonment for murder and 99 years for kidnapping. The sentence was a stiff one, but through the efforts of Mr. Darrow and Judge Caverly, a small element of humanity had been salvaged. Murder was not to be compounded by murder.

Then there was the Snyder-Gray case, equally chilling but entirely different:

The Albert Snyder house in Queens Village, New York, was much like that of any other comfortable American family. Shaded by trees, meticulously maintained, it housed Albert Snyder, art editor of the magazine *Motor Boating,* his mother-in-law and his daughter. It was also home to his wife, Ruth, a woman who was to become a household word, although she hadn't intended it that way.

All she wanted to do was to murder her husband, whom she had heavily insured without his knowledge. Two efforts to do him in with gas had failed. The third attempt—a brutal bludgeoning compounded by other diabolical goings on— took care of gentle Albert Snyder. In the bargain, it took care also of Ruth Snyder and her lover, Judd Gray.

As Alexander Woollcott put it, and that corpulent gentleman had a way with words:

> "Ruth Snyder was so like the woman across the street that many an American husband was soon haunted by the realization that she also bore an embarrassing resemblance to the woman across the breakfast table."

Not exactly a cheery thought for the American male to ponder.

This middle-class house, and the actions of the middle-class woman who lived there, came close to eclipsing the really big stories of 1927: Lindbergh's dramatic crossing and the ordeals of Sacco and Vanzetti. This was a case which hit close to home—too close for comfort.

At issue was the murder of Albert Snyder by his wife, Ruth, and her boy friend, Judd Gray, a traveling salesman in corsetry, who made time with Ruth when he had the opportunity.

As a murder, it was badly handled. As a burning emotional issue, it could not have been better contrived if Cecil B. DeMille had been running the show. On a March Sunday, as Snyder lay sleeping, his devoted wife—32, well built and attractive—and her married lover, battered Albert with a sash weight, chloroformed him, choked him and tied a wire around his neck. They were taking no further chances with the gas jet in this final attempt. Snyder, was, of course, dead.

The pair was not to enjoy unfettered existence for long. Attempts to feign burglary and assault were so naïve as to bring doubts to the mind of a six-year-old of semi-moderate intelligence.

The trial for murder began within a month, to considerable press coverage and ogling, reminiscent of another famous crime of the Twenties—the Hall-Mills case.

The guilty duo confessed in rich detail and proceeded to hang themselves, as it were, despite the best efforts of Mrs. Snyder's attorney, who tried to portray his client as devoted to her husband, home and child. It was this facet of her character—her very ordinariness—which captured the country's imagination and probably prompted Mr. Woollcott's previously cited observation.

The attorney, Edgar F. Hazelton, also attempted to prove that in actuality Snyder himself was at fault through creating a loveless atmosphere in which Ruth could neither survive nor function.

Everyone wanted to get into the act. Aimee Semple McPherson, her own reputation marred by scandal, rose to the fore to implore young men to take up the credo: "I want a wife like mother—not a red hot cutie."

Meanwhile, true love cooled. Judd Gray blamed the episode on Mrs. Snyder, with the cooperation of his lawyers, Samuel L. Miller and William J. Millard, who tried to picture him as an innocent, misled by the evil Ruth. Mrs. Snyder retaliated that the crime was actually the brainchild of her hapless lover, Judd.

The end was in sight. After 9 minutes of deliberation, the two were found guilty. Two and one half years after their liaison had begun, Snyder and Gray were together again upon, it is said, adjoining slabs in the Sing Sing morgue.

But togetherness was never as important as money to Ruth Snyder. At the time of her electrocution, she was still suing her insurance company for the $96,000 they had, for some reason, refused to pay her upon the death of her husband.

For the gossipmonger, the sensation seeker, and the muckraker, there was plenty to talk about in the years that spanned the War and the Depression. In addition to Leopold and Loeb and Snyder-Gray, there was also the Hall-Mills trial, which long dominated dubious conversation.

It all began in 1922, when Edward Wheeler Hall, pastor of St. John the Evangelist Church of New Brunswick, New Jersey, was found shot to death under a crabapple tree on a farm near the city.

That a clergyman should be so discovered was titillating in itself. What whetted the appetites of the prurient even more was that the Reverend was not alone. Found dead at his side was one Mrs. James (Eleanor) Mills, a singer in the choir of Hall's church, where her husband was employed as sexton. Near the two of them were found passionately compromising love letters which they, themselves, had obviously written unless they were extremely competent forgeries.

With such evidence of infidelity, the now-widowed Mrs. Hall and her family were the obvious suspects in the case. There was certainly a motive. Because of the almost automatic suspicion, and due to sloppiness and bickering on the part of the police, the actual killers have, to this day, not been found.

Initially, Mrs. Hall and her brothers, Willie and Henry Stevens, escaped indictment by a grand jury. The case was not pursued. The whole mess seemed to have been forgotten except, of course, for the absence of the murderers.

So matters stood until 1926, when a newspaperman named Philip Payne was fired from his job at the New York *Daily News.* On the professional rebound, and almost immediately ensconced as managing editor of the New York *Mirror,* Payne launched a vendetta against his former paper. His goal was not only to equal but to surpass the circulation of the *News*—a formidable task. In order to bring about this *coup,* he sought a target that would grab the imagination of the reading public.

Inspired, perhaps, by theatre-goers' reactions to the 1922 production of *Rain,* starring Jeanne Eagels as the passionate Sadie Thompson who seduced an innocent missionary (at least this was a theory of critic Alexander Woollcott), Philip Payne found ammunition for re-entry into the big time.

Possessed with monumental gall, which was backed by little evidence, he turned the *Mirror's* attention back four years to the all-but-forgotten Lovers' Lane mystery.

Alleging that Mrs. Hall's family had stood in the way of earlier investigation, Payne, through repeated editorial prodding convinced the New Jersey authorities that Mrs. Hall should be indicted for the murders of her husband and his lady friend. She duly was.

The trial which followed dominated the columns of all of the Metropolitan papers, including those of *The New York Times* which appeared to consider the resulting legal asininity "fit to print." Over 300 reporters were in attendance, and even James Mills, husband of the dead woman, signed on as a paid newspaper "observer."

Actually, the only prosecution witness of note was Jane Gibson, dubbed by the press as the "Pig Woman," who testified from her bed. Although seriously ill with cancer, she was duly hauled into the court room for the unusual testimony that she had heard the shots that killed the two and had fleetingly seen the defendants while taking a midnight ride on her mule, Jenny. Spectacular as it was, her statement did not stand up in court. Why, for instance, had she not sought help after witnessing a scene of violence? Jane Gibson could not answer.

After weeks of ballyhoo, reflecting badly on the United States judicial system and the press which covered the nonsense in copious detail, Frances Stevens Hall and her two brothers were acquitted.

Quietly, and out of court, the defendants accepted a libel settlement from the *Mirror* of $50,000—an event hardly noted in the abashed press. As for Payne, he was lost the following year in an abortive attempt to fly the Atlantic Ocean.

The famous "Monkey Trial" was quite a different kind of proceeding. The trial of John Thomas Scopes for teaching *The Origin of the Species* (Charles Darwin's theory of evolution) was not so much a test of Scopes, himself, but a conflict between the Old Thinking, as personified by William Jennings Bryan, and the New Thinking, summed up in the personality of Clarence Darrow. These two renowned attorneys represented the conflict of fundamentalist religion and a scientifically based intellectuality.

A glance at any current newspaper should prove that these rival forces are still battling each other. Accept on faith— have faith in reason: these are our options.

As most people now know, the case of Scopes vs. the people of Tennessee was a put-up job, with the enlightened biologist offering himself up as a sacrificial lamb in order to prove a point. His agreement to do so was delivered some weeks before the trial at an informal meeting in Robinson's Drugstore in Dayton, Tennessee.

What happened in addition to the carnival that took place— lemonade stands, hot dog pushers, stunt men, Bible hawkers, the press and all manner of hangers-on flocked to Dayton for the big show— was a choosing up of sides (rationality or emotionalism?). Neither faction can be said to have really won the case. The clash is continuing until this day.

The climax of doctrinal differences occurred in the summer of 1925. The Tennessee legislature, dominated by the fundamentalists, passed a new law: "It shall be unlawful for any teacher in any of the . . . public schools of the State, which are supported in whole or in part by the public school funds of the State, to teach any theory that denies the story of the Divine creation of man as taught in the Bible, and to teach instead that man has descended from a lower order of animals."

John T. Scopes accepted the proposition that he, at age 24, with his full career ahead of him, should allow himself to be caught teaching Darwin to his students. Upon his arrest, which was a foregone conclusion, William Jennings Bryan offered his services to the state. The Civil Liberties Union retained the aging Clarence Darrow for the defense. The fight was on. Bryan was the "conservative," Darrow the "radical"—although in 1971 his ideas do not seem to be particularly left of center.

The press poured into Dayton, Tennessee. Requests for

"The eclipse is very much like the defeat of the Democratic Party. It is only temporary and the sun will soon shine again." William Jennings Bryan remarked upon the election of Calvin Coolidge. Perhaps he also believed that, if ignored, the theory of Evolution would disappear.

trial coverage came in from Europe and Asia. If it was true that the City fathers desired the trial in order to put Dayton on the map, they were getting their wish.

Signs similar to those that bedecked Dayton during that long, hot summer can be seen today along the roads of the Deep South: "Prepare to Meet Thy Maker," "Where Will YOU Spend Eternity?"

Along with the influx of big city people came the country folk, often not knowing what was at issue, but feeling threatened, wanting to find out, to understand, the thinking of the Great Big World outside of Dayton, Tennessee. And to preserve the attitudes of a lifetime.

Court was opened with a prayer. Everyone from Judge John T. Raulston, to the defendant, to the courtly Mr. Bryan, shed his coat. From the beginning, the atmosphere was decidedly against Darrow and his client. The learned scientists whom the attorney had imported to testify in Scopes' behalf received short shrift from Judge Raulston. Indeed, His Honor made his preference explicit when he chose to refer to Bryan and his assistants as "generals" and Darrow and his as "colonels."

That Darrow was able to survive in this hostile place, in which the Judge's preconceptions of human life beginning

The last ordeal for William Jennings Bryan occurred in Dayton, Tennessee in 1925. Five days after the Scopes trial ended, the Great Commoner was dead.

with Adam were obvious, is yet another testimony to his brilliance. In a master stroke, he called upon Bryan himself to take the witness stand as a Biblical scholar. In the exchange that followed, Bryan became less and less comfortable. Darrow's always penetrating questions had become more and more difficult for the famous barrister and politician to handle. In near hysteria, William Jennings Bryan accused Clarence Darrow of coming to Tennessee not to defend Scopes, but to repudiate orthodox Christianity. Eve's virtue, or lack of it, was thrown into the melee and Bryan answered, as he often did, "The Bible states it; it must be so."

With all of Darrow's knowledge and insight, the verdict was assured. Scopes was found guilty and fined $100. But despite the verdict, momentous events were to come about:

Bryan was attacked by the press in general, violently by Henry L. Mencken, by the intellectuals of both coasts and middle America. All of these found the "Great Commoner" in error. Five days after the close of the strenuous trial, William Jennings Bryan was dead.

Scopes lived on for many years—into an age that could embrace Clarence Darrow and praise the humble, courageous school teacher from Tennessee for what he saw, what he did and what he risked.

The Scopes Trial was a battle of ideas.

The case of Daddy and Peaches Browning would bring a blush to the cheek of Vladimir Naboakov. When that novelist wrote *Lolita,* he described the love of aging Humbert Humbert for his nymphet as a journey into understanding as well as passion. Daddy and Peaches never stopped to understand. What this elderly gentleman and his barely nubile wife had going for them has never been revealed. Maybe Peaches had an Oedipus complex. Maybe Daddy was attempting to prove a fading virility. But this is idle conjecture.

Daddy and his baby came to the astonished attention of America in the mid-twenties. It was in 1926 that Daddy discovered his prize, born Frances Belle Heenan, a school girl from Washington Heights—and proceeded to shower her with flowers and other gifts until the 15-year-old girl was thoroughly smitten with her suitor of 51.

On April 10 they were married, attracting the attention of the omnipresent press to the extent that they would be followed and harrassed throughout their brief marriage. By early October, the fuzz was off the Peach, the marriage was on the rocks, and the tabloids were in their tasteless element. The story even made page one of *The New York Times.* In this troubled world, it seems beyond belief that anyone really *cared* about the marital problems of this odd couple, yet it seems that everyone did.

Each employed a ghost writer to tell his side of the story to the sensationalist press, and every written word fell on avid ears.

While Daddy claimed that Peaches suffered from a mother obsession which had ruined their chances for happiness from the beginning, his bride allowed as how her husband had insisted upon nudity at the breakfast table and had cavorted about the bedroom in similar attire.

Daddy won the suit for separation which left him without a wife but otherwise unaffected. Peaches, herself, was left without a sou. Capitalizing on her dubious fame, she entered vaudeville. When Daddy died in 1934 she claimed, and collected, a widow's share of his estate. In 1956—three marriages and three divorces from Washington Heights—the juvenile sensation of the Jazz Age was dead from a fall in the bath tub. She was 46 years old, and still looking for whatever it was she never found.

Right—Proud papa with his barely nubile bride (although she had something going for her). Daddy Browning, and his devoted wife, "Peaches."

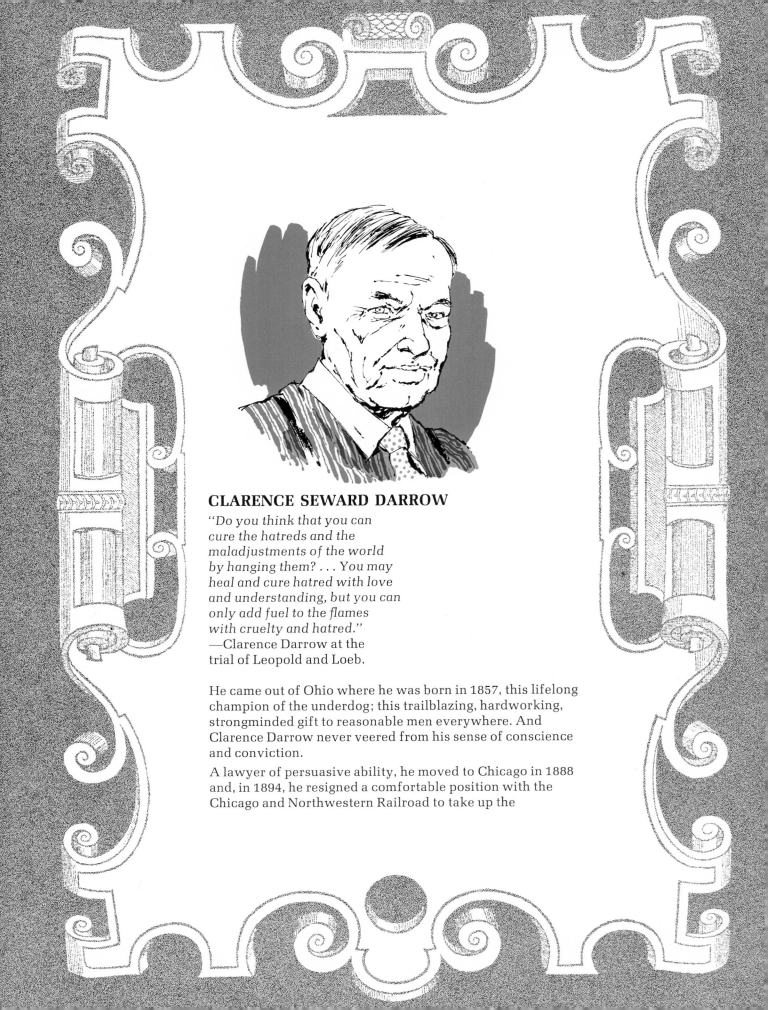

CLARENCE SEWARD DARROW

"Do you think that you can cure the hatreds and the maladjustments of the world by hanging them? . . . You may heal and cure hatred with love and understanding, but you can only add fuel to the flames with cruelty and hatred."
—Clarence Darrow at the trial of Leopold and Loeb.

He came out of Ohio where he was born in 1857, this lifelong champion of the underdog; this trailblazing, hardworking, strongminded gift to reasonable men everywhere. And Clarence Darrow never veered from his sense of conscience and conviction.

A lawyer of persuasive ability, he moved to Chicago in 1888 and, in 1894, he resigned a comfortable position with the Chicago and Northwestern Railroad to take up the

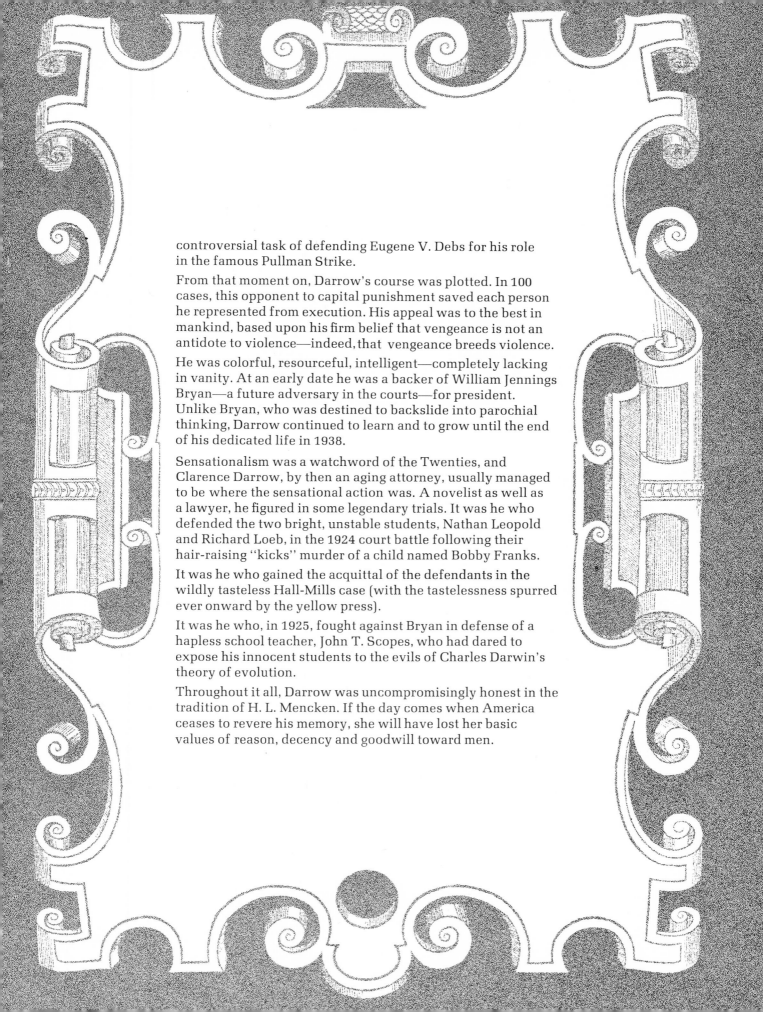

controversial task of defending Eugene V. Debs for his role in the famous Pullman Strike.

From that moment on, Darrow's course was plotted. In 100 cases, this opponent to capital punishment saved each person he represented from execution. His appeal was to the best in mankind, based upon his firm belief that vengeance is not an antidote to violence—indeed, that vengeance breeds violence.

He was colorful, resourceful, intelligent—completely lacking in vanity. At an early date he was a backer of William Jennings Bryan—a future adversary in the courts—for president. Unlike Bryan, who was destined to backslide into parochial thinking, Darrow continued to learn and to grow until the end of his dedicated life in 1938.

Sensationalism was a watchword of the Twenties, and Clarence Darrow, by then an aging attorney, usually managed to be where the sensational action was. A novelist as well as a lawyer, he figured in some legendary trials. It was he who defended the two bright, unstable students, Nathan Leopold and Richard Loeb, in the 1924 court battle following their hair-raising "kicks" murder of a child named Bobby Franks.

It was he who gained the acquittal of the defendants in the wildly tasteless Hall-Mills case (with the tastelessness spurred ever onward by the yellow press).

It was he who, in 1925, fought against Bryan in defense of a hapless school teacher, John T. Scopes, who had dared to expose his innocent students to the evils of Charles Darwin's theory of evolution.

Throughout it all, Darrow was uncompromisingly honest in the tradition of H. L. Mencken. If the day comes when America ceases to revere his memory, she will have lost her basic values of reason, decency and goodwill toward men.

WILLIAM JENNINGS BRYAN

*"He came into life a hero,
A Galahad, in bright and
shining armor. He was passing
out a poor mountebank."*
—H. L. Mencken

William Jennings Bryan's life was studded with contradictions. Fiercely handsome, the onetime "Prairie Radical" ended his days as a defender of the *status quo*. The last great trial of his life—the celebrated "Monkey Trial"—moved the "great commoner" to invoke the wrath of Hell against the forces of logical thought. An intelligent man, Bryan nevertheless could not reconcile the discoveries of science with the revelations of the Bible.

Born in Illinois in 1860 and educated as a lawyer, Bryan established himself in Lincoln, Nebraska and served four years in Congress before becoming editor-in-chief of the Omaha *World Herald*. In 1896, still very young as such things go, he received the Democratic and Populist nominations for President—although conservative Democrats loudly opposed him. The election was lost to William McKinley, the Republican candidate.

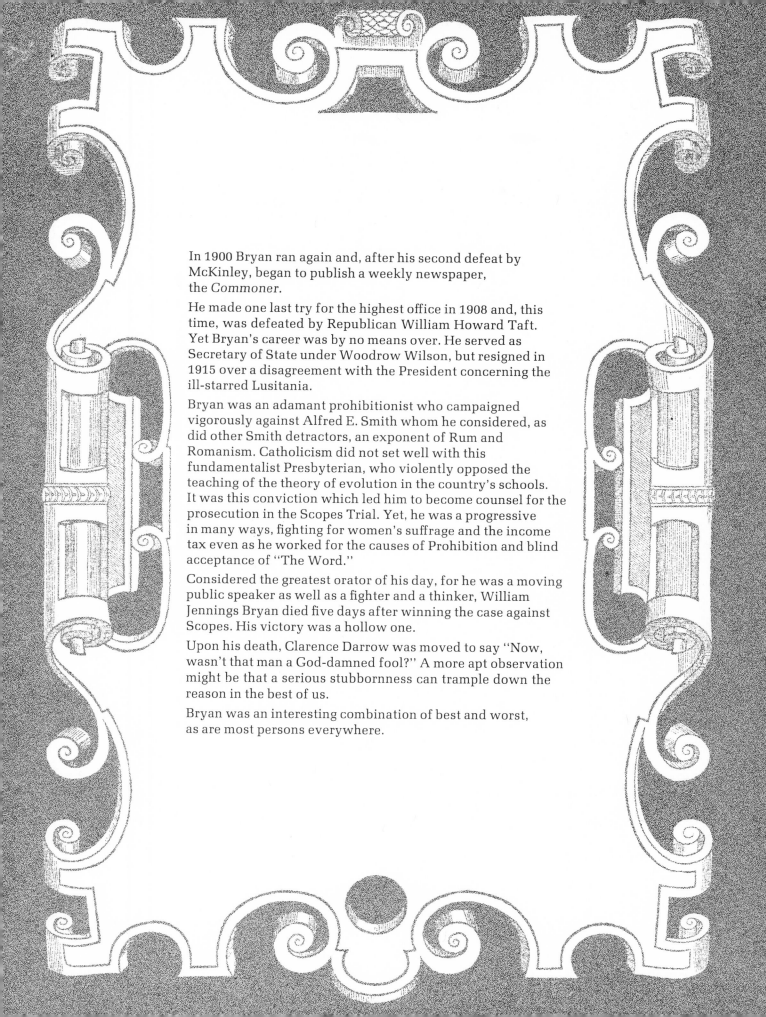

In 1900 Bryan ran again and, after his second defeat by McKinley, began to publish a weekly newspaper, the *Commoner*.

He made one last try for the highest office in 1908 and, this time, was defeated by Republican William Howard Taft. Yet Bryan's career was by no means over. He served as Secretary of State under Woodrow Wilson, but resigned in 1915 over a disagreement with the President concerning the ill-starred Lusitania.

Bryan was an adamant prohibitionist who campaigned vigorously against Alfred E. Smith whom he considered, as did other Smith detractors, an exponent of Rum and Romanism. Catholicism did not set well with this fundamentalist Presbyterian, who violently opposed the teaching of the theory of evolution in the country's schools. It was this conviction which led him to become counsel for the prosecution in the Scopes Trial. Yet, he was a progressive in many ways, fighting for women's suffrage and the income tax even as he worked for the causes of Prohibition and blind acceptance of "The Word."

Considered the greatest orator of his day, for he was a moving public speaker as well as a fighter and a thinker, William Jennings Bryan died five days after winning the case against Scopes. His victory was a hollow one.

Upon his death, Clarence Darrow was moved to say "Now, wasn't that man a God-damned fool?" A more apt observation might be that a serious stubbornness can trample down the reason in the best of us.

Bryan was an interesting combination of best and worst, as are most persons everywhere.

CHAPTER SIX

Boys Meet Girls
and
Girls Meet Life

It was a time of cultural revolution, a revolution which affected nearly everyone, but most of all the ladies.

Suffrage was a reality at last, and with the right to vote woman took her first tentative steps to regarding herself as man's equal. She was ready to cast aside an ancient code of feminine "purity," to discard the homely niche in which she'd been placed, to step from the pedestal upon which she had long reposed.

Advertising, an industry always looking for more and better markets, sensed this spirit of change and illustrated it in almost subliminal ways. Women weren't actually pictured smoking cigarettes, not at the beginning, but through the use of the female presence in previously all-male cigarette advertising, women were encouraged to experience the delights of the wicked weed. It seems a minor thing, but it was a portent of what was to come.

For decades woman had occupied an inferior position in the social structure. Yet, at the same time, she was supposed to maintain a kind of moral superiority. She was expected to uphold society's ethical values, as an example to her daughters, as an inspiration to her sons and husbands, as protector of the family morality. And she was to accomplish all this out of some superior inner strength and with a knowledge of a world sealed out by the four walls of her kitchen.

Her resolution to abide by this double standard came from a steely will for self-sacrifice and, sometimes, from a desire to be "taken care of"—a desire anything but inborn but carefully planted in her by men, and by the mothers and grandmothers who had long since been indoctrinated by the "system."

Men, of course, had always been encouraged to "sow their oats"—with those lower-class ladies who professed to enjoy a sexual experience which went beyond a romantic kiss beneath the lilac bush. It was commonly assumed that women who enjoyed sex were on a lower level than alley cats. Masters and Johnson weren't around in those halcyon days to assert that woman's sexual drive equals or surpasses that of man. There had been few psychological studies to indicate that most prostitutes did (and do) tend to be frigid and often homosexual.

Through the end of World War I a "nice girl" was a "nice girl"—the embodiment of modesty and decorum— and that was that.

Irene Castle may have started it all, but soon everyone was doing it.
The Flapper, like Samson, was duly shorn.

When eyebrows began to lift at skirts wafting a full nine inches above the floor, at the use of cosmetics, at cheek-to-cheek dancing, the mothers and fathers of America sensed, however vaguely, that there was a full scale rebellion going on—a rebellion which had nothing to do with Bolshevism but which was even more threatening at the grass roots of society.

F. Scott Fitzgerald brought the whole thing into focus in *This Side of Paradise*. With its publication the worst fears of the older generation were confirmed. So "petting parties" did indeed exist, and not just in the wicked urban centers of New York and Chicago. Increased speed in communication, through radio and syndicated newspaper columns, was to see to that. So girls "kissed dozens of men." Anguished discussion of what was happening to America's daughters proliferated across the land. Nearly everyone was worried—except, of course, the young ladies themselves who were beginning to experience and enjoy their new freedoms.

Most of the clergy deplored the new trends. Leaders of society clamored for a return to propriety. The good women of the YWCA came forth with a campaign for reform in feminine dress, a campaign backed up by the conservative legislatures of several states.

To some, Charleston means a genteel southern city. To the flapper it meant a dance, raucous as it was innocent, frequently shocking to the elders of the day.

The whole thing smacked of a nasty modernity. Few of the older generation stopped to recall that the ladies of Louis XIV's court were noted for their décolletage, as their counterparts of today are unwilling to admit that such sterling characters as Thomas Jefferson and Benjamin Franklin wore long hair and that this is a fashion which was probably shared by Jesus Christ and Moses.

Things were changing for many reasons. World War I, which had brought death and anxiety close to the cloistered young, created a climate of eat, drink and be merry that did not abate with the signing of the armistice. Exposure to Europe's "evil" ways had proved that one can't go home again to a world that no longer exists in one's personal value system.

There was a feeling, shared by the youth of today, that one's elders had pretty well botched the job and that, therefore, their standards and mores were not necessarily right or to be emulated.

And if philosophical existence had become more complicated, physical existence was increasingly easy. Women were to find that housekeeping was not the all-consuming task it had been before electric power was a common force in the home, before canned goods and delicatessens made meal preparation a great deal simpler than it had been, before ready-to-wear clothes were available in department stores and corner shops.

And, thus, was Prohibition guaranteed.

The feminine tippler does her thing, circa 1922. A flask, concealed within her boots, holds an evening's supply of giggly.

Standing in the background was the ominous presence of
Sigmund Freud. While he, himself, was not particularly
liberated, although he insisted upon treating his own wife
as a cherished chattel, not unlike the trapped Nora of Ibsen's
A Doll's House, he had, through his pioneering work, made
sex an acceptable topic of conversation and analysis a
fashionable enterprise.
Add to this the omnipresent automobile, the farce of
Prohibition, and there was little for Mama and Papa to do
but sit back in horror and witness the evolution of

The Flapper

*"There was a young woman
Who lived in a 'Speak,'
When presented with gin,
she said 'Gracious, that's weak!'
So she added a soupcon of
wood alcohol
And, when asked if it harmed
her said
'Why no, not at all.'"*
—Anonymous

Not all of the young ladies of the 1920s were quite as daring
as the damsel quoted in the foregoing bit of doggerel.
But some of them were, and the actions of those were the
stuff from which pipe dreams were made.

Fashionable Manhattan ladies gained a tobacco emporium of their own when a
certain Mme. Charciel (above) opened her strictly female "Smoke Parlor"
on E. 72nd Street. Cigarettes were available to match clothing, coiffure or skin tone.

John O'Hara, always a great one for sticking pins in overly inflated balloons, knew what the "flapper" really was: not a chic, short-haired, short-skirted, whisky-belting little thing at all. In one of his later short stories, O'Hara cited "flapper" as British slang for the unmarried post-debutante.

Putting it crudely, she was a girl just "flapping around" until her Prince Charming should make the scene and carry her off to bliss and rapture—on his white horse or in his flivver. So much for etymology.

The "flapper" as characterized by artist John Held and writer F. Scott Fitzgerald, was the with-it personification of the Jazz Age. Just by doing her own thing, Twenties style, she became a national heroine to the young and uninhibited. To be sure, Mrs. Grundy clucked into her snuff box at the flapper's antics, but college boys adored her.

Her setting was the speak-easy or the country club or the Model T. Her milieu was the necking and/or petting party. She defied her mother, often smoked, carried a flask of whisky or gin secured by her rolled-down garter.

She knew the latest dance steps, was frequently quoted in uttering such hitherto "no-no's" as "hell" or "damn" in mixed company. (And the company in which she moved was usually mixed.) She had a superficial knowledge of Freud—and, maybe, Jung and Adler—and was said to carry condoms in her compact. Sometimes she did—but not always. As with many renegades, her behavior was often expressed in talk rather than in action.

Holding her liquor like a man, the prohibition-bred young woman frequented the hitherto *verboten* saloons. And she enjoyed them.

She bound her breasts, not to decrease her femininity, but to show the boys that she was a companion, a playmate, and not merely a cosseted hothouse plant. She had her hair bobbed because there wasn't time, what with all the endless hullabaloo, to worry over pins and rats. Was this the forerunner of unisex? She wore her skirts above the knee, and her stockings below the knee as an expression of her emerging emancipation from the coal stove and sock darning.

That the flapper existed, galoshes and all, cannot be disputed. That she was ubiquitous most certainly can. Whether she was Held's invention or he her faithful reflector still remains in some doubt.

For every girl who shed her confining corset, a dozen others wore them still—sometimes through personal choice, sometimes through the prodding of indignant female relatives. And those who complied with the wishes of their families often were rid of the detested garments as soon as they departed the familial hearth. For every girl who questioned the values in which she had been reared, there were a dozen others clinging to the haven of the home as though World War I had been as meaningful as a comic strip. For every girl who attempted to translate the world around her into Freudian terms, there were the sweet little fundamentalist maidens devoting their unawakened passions to God and Country in the church choirs of the nation.

But, the youthful revolutionaries of the Twenties were sowing seeds which would take root and blossom as the

These champions of an earlier peace movement petitioned President Harding to grant amnesty for political prisoners some 50 years ago.

decades passed: seeds of self-expression, revolt from the ideas and ideals of a generation which to them seemed hopelessly archaic.

As is almost axiomatic, for all of those who revolted in active displeasure from the tenor of Victorian times, there were those absorbing some of the new culture, some of the new values, in quiet and reflection, without subscribing to, or participating in, every iconoclastic gesture.

Today's feminine hippie, dripping love beads and philosophising in sometimes profound, often contradictory terms, is different from the flapper only in the direction her rebellion takes. While the nonconformist of today deplores opulent chic because it has long been acceptable to her mother, her counterpart of fifty years ago espoused it.
It was a welcome antidote to the war, to an era of almost totally unrelieved dowdiness.

The flapper focussed in upon herself, while the love child admits to concern about the entirety of humanity. Which is the more self-indulgent? One seemed to care too little, the other seems to care too much. Then, as now, shocking one's elders was a favorite avocation of the young.

Mrs. Grundy's opinion was already losing its importance. We can hope that before this decade is out, it will, like the good, be interred with her bones.

The Flapper, for all her hedonism, started it all.
Where would Ti-Grace Atkinson be today if it hadn't been for the Twenties?

An outcome of Prohibition not anticipated by the WCTU—the dolls joining the guys for a spot of gin.

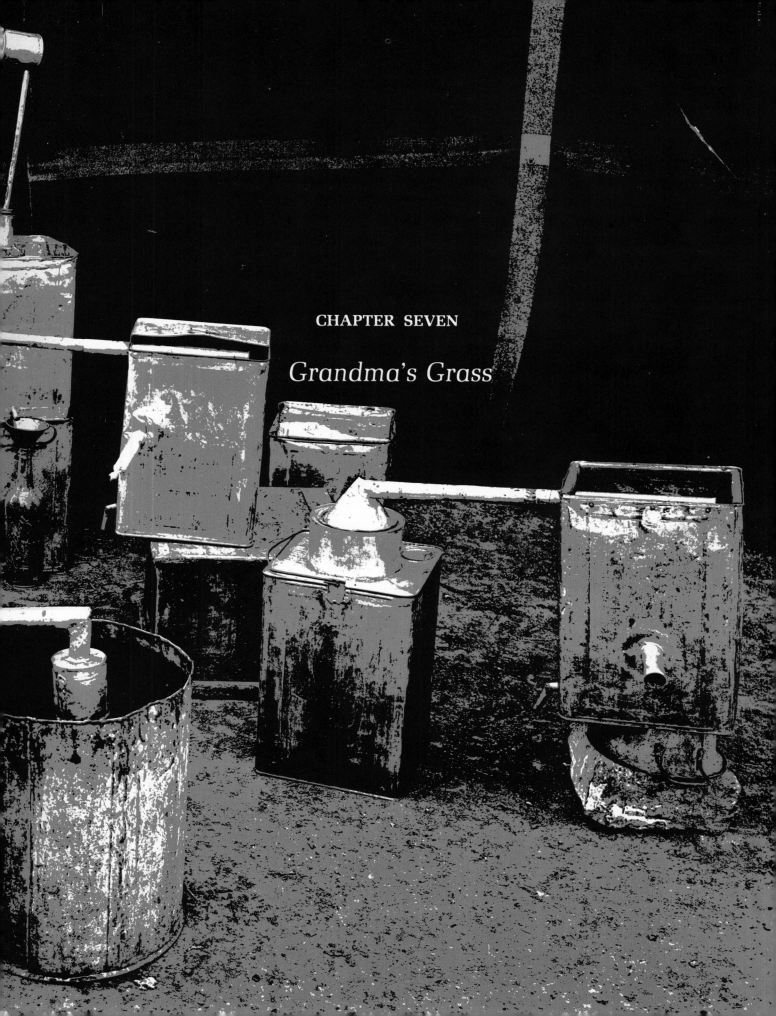

CHAPTER SEVEN

Grandma's Grass

The noble experiment of Prohibition did little to enoble American society.

When Warren Gamaliel Harding took up his lax rein on the hold of the nation, the Eighteenth Amendment—Prohibition —had, for eight months, been a part of the Constitution of the United States. The Volstead Act, designed to enforce this unrealistic new law had been passed by Congress over the veto of President Woodrow Wilson, and had gone into effect at midnight, January 16, 1920. Harding, anything but a ''dry'' himself, regarded the law as a mandate from the people and, whatever his private doubts, attempted to enforce it.

When Governor Alfred E. Smith's New York legislature sought to repeal the amendment in that state, Harding issued a warning[1] to the Happy Warrior—a warning deeply resented by many of the Empire State's citizens, as an example of demagoguery. Harding said, in part:

> ''The nation has deliberately, after many years of consideration, adopted the present policy, which is written into the Eighteenth Amendment. It is the law of the land and of every state within the Union. So long as it remains the national policy, there can be only one course for the national government to pursue. That is to use every means to make effective the law passed in compliance with this constitutional mandate.
> To do this will be the unquestioning policy of the present Administration. . . .''

Whether the president then retired for a pleasant Scotch and soda with his cronies is not known. Actually, the whole thing had been unworkable from the start, regardless of the protestations of the WCTU, the Anti-saloon League, and the tirelessly fulminating Billy Sunday.

''John Barleycorn'' did not die with the enactment of the Eighteenth Amendment. He simply went underground for a while, taking with him a vast percentage of the nation's men —and its women. Federal agents deployed to halt the sales of alcohol (except for medicinal dosages, prescribed by physicians and available from pharmacies) had no more luck with that dubious enterprise than they are having today in their efforts to prevent the use and possession of marijuana. Drinking was not about to fade away with the demise of the corner saloon. In fact, it was to become more fashionable than ever, for both sexes.

[1]The statement was issued on May 16, 1923.

It was a foolish and ill-conceived law, an attempt to legislate personal morality and, as such, enforcement was impossible. The most tragic result was the increasing public disregard for all the laws of the land—a growing recognition of the fallibility of government which exists unto the present day within the minds of many.

It was a law destined to foster cynicism in all but the most conservative souls, as it was continuously flaunted, ignored, and disobeyed. It was a law which encouraged many with records of good citizenship into the illegal world of the bootleggers, both to sell and to purchase. It was a law which put the average citizen into contact with the underworld. It was a law which interfered with personal freedom and was, therefore, to be scoffed at by a people who considered themselves free. Everybody scoffed.

And nearly everybody drank: wine, beer, spirits. It didn't seem to matter.

There was liquor to be had—almost everywhere—in the speak-easies that prevailed in every city of the nation in astonishing numbers, or delivered to one's door, or purchased from carefully secreted moonshine distilleries.

The nation's capital, seat of the enforcers of prohibition, was not immune from the ubiquitous still. This one, with a 500 gallon capacity, was taken along with mash, rifles, revolvers and 1000 rounds of ammunition.

The country was awash within a sea of booze; booze from Canada, booze from England, booze created in the privacy of one's personal bathtub. Much of it was of poor quality, not infrequently it was watered down, almost always it was overpriced.

Open defiance of a provision of the Constitution caused a new wave of anxiety and guilt, but never mind all that—another sip from the trusty flask and everything would seem all right again (at least until the hangover set in). Judging from the contents of some of those spirited bottles, some of the hangovers must have been monumental.

The Coast Guard worked overtime to see that the rumrunners did not penetrate the three mile limit and its diligent efforts caused not a few of the runners to give up the ghost. Still, a great many of them got through. Rowboats, motor launches, every conceivable sort of seaworthy craft went out to meet the smuggler's ships. Smuggling was a profitable business, if one were not caught.

What developed was an atmosphere in which gangsterism, graft and corruption had plenty of breathing room, an atmosphere that seemed almost unreal, seen as it often was through the haze of illicit liquor or from the smoky mustiness of the nearest Speak.

The high cost of drinking—and this from a rum-runner's poop deck.

It was chic to break the law. So the chicest duos in the major cities visited the Speakeasies, spent their money, and nursed their hangovers.

While the idle rich clipped coupons and the better speaks clipped the idle rich, the poor endured intolerable conditions in this, the land of affluence.

Deep in the heart of Texas Guinan's posh speakeasy, paying guests admire
Miss Guinan (center) and the star of the evening (somewhat horsey).

Former wine drinkers turned to the cocktail, a more potent potable generally available in speak-easies. Frequently the police themselves collaborated with the perpetrators of the insidious brews—although there were law enforcement agents, among them Izzy Einstein and Moe Smith, who pursued their calling with almost legendary ingenuity.

There simply wasn't the personnel required to adequately protect our seacoasts and the lengthy stretch of the Canadian border which stretches for nearly 4,000 miles. If every prohibition violator had been caught in the act, there would not have been the jails to contain them. And everybody knew it.

Fiorello LaGuardia, then a Congressman from New York, ventured that it would require a quarter of a million law enforcement agents to oversee the Volstead Act in New York City alone.

Nearly 1,000 cases of beer meet an ignoble end at the hands of Prohibition agents. What a waste of money and time.

"LIBERTY, LIBERTY—WHERE HAVE I HEARD THAT WORD BEFORE? WASN'T IT THE NAME OF A STATUE OR SOMETHING?"

In one of the more shocking revelations of the decade, it was disclosed that Senator Morris Sheppard of Texas, author of the notorious amendment, was producing about 130 gallons of whisky a day in a still located on his own farm.

Small wonder that the law was rarely followed—although there were exceptions. The author's grandfather, an almost saintly individual who, into his ninetieth year, remained moderate almost to the point of abstention, returned from France after World War I with two cases of superb Burgundy. On January 16, 1920, as a champion of the American Constitution (although not particularly of Mr. Harding), grandfather drained all 24 precious bottles into the kitchen sink. To him, the law was the law, even if the law were ridiculous—and he thought it was.

For those with iron-clad stomachs and penchants for the strong stuff, there was always a still and a supplier.

There were others like him—but there was money to be made from Prohibition—money to be made by the likes of Al Capone, who grossed millions from the debacle. After all, who was to stop him?

Out of Prohibition grew some of New York's better restaurants: 21 and the now defunct, but lamented, Stork Club among them—spas later to become favorite watering places of cafe and show-business society. There were the other Speaks that did not survive into the Thirties and legalized consumption of alcohol: Texas Guinan's, Belle Livingston's, the House of (Helen) Morgan. In 1929, official "greeter" Grover Whelan estimated that 32,000 such houses of pleasure existed in New York City. There are many who believe that the figure was inordinately low.

Anonymity carefully preserved, a gaggle of otherwise respectable gentlemen diligently break the law in a Jazz Age Speakeasy.

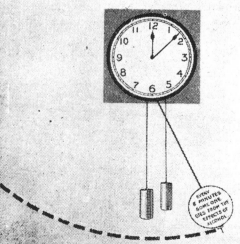

The selling of liquor wasn't a going concern in New York and Chicago alone. This operation of dispensing liquor and dodging the "Feds" reached into every corner of the nation, into swank night spots and into rural stills. Some places provided only set-ups, others served gin in tea cups. Those whose owners paid off properly, to the police and to the mobs, often served *bona fide* drinks in crystal glasses with real ice cubes.

As drinking became illegal, it became unusually chic—just as "pot" is becoming in our currently troubled decade.

Prohibition was a farce that appears to have brought out the worst in practically everybody because:

Long before the advent of the rumrunners, those who espoused prohibition had missed the philosophical boat. There is an enormous distinction to be drawn between *abstinence* and *temperance*. To take Daddy out of the saloon at night and return him, safe and sober, to his worrying family was the primary purpose of the Drys. To confuse the despair and ravages of drunkenness with a glass of champagne at a wedding, a bottle of Bordeaux with dinner, or a connubially shared nightcap was a major mistake.

In their misdirected zeal to eliminate the horrors of Skid Row, starving children and hysterical wives, the Prohibitionists created the kind of obsession with drink and drinking that could come about only through such legislation. More drunkenness was to come about *because* of Prohibition than ever occurred before its institution.

All there was left to endure was the terrible Crash of 1929, the election of Franklin Delano Roosevelt, and, finally, the only sensible move possible under the circumstances: repeal.

Just another Speak.

NOT TRANSFERABLE   VOLUNTEER 8307

Odeon Club
41 EAST 53rd STREET
NEW YORK

FLM

N⁰   150

ALCOHOLISM and DEGENERATION.

(Permission Scientific Temperance Federation.)

Investigation of Twenty Families made by PROF. DEMME, of Bern, 1878-1889.

Descendants of Ten VERY Temperate Families.	Descendants of Ten IN-Temperate Families.
NORMAL	**NORMAL**

50 normal children out of 61 children	Only 10 normal children out of 57 children
DEFORMED	**DEFORMED**

2 children out of 61	5 deformed children out of 57
ACKWARD MENTAL DEVELOPMENT (NOT IDIOTIC)	**DWARFED**

Only 2 children out of 61	5 dwarfed children out of 57
ST. VITUS' DANCE	**EPILEPTIC**

	5 epileptic children out of 57
	IDIOTIC
Only 2 deformed children out of 61	7 idiotic children out of 57
DIED IN INFANCY	**DIED IN INFANCY**

nly 5 children died in infancy out of 61	25 children died in infancy out of 57

ALPHONSE CAPONE

"All for Al and Al for All!"
—Capone mob rallying cry

Johnny Torrio disliked competition. In the early days of Prohibition, the Chicago-based gangster recognized that the city would pay well for its liquor—that there was a fortune to be made. But he recognized also that free-enterprise rum-running could be the death of his dreams of glory.

What was needed was a strongarm man of parts. To get him, Torrio, a onetime member of the Five Points gang of New York, turned to his native territory. It was in Brooklyn that he discovered Al Capone, a lowly dishwasher, with credentials in the use of the blackjack and other weapons. In World War I, Capone had become familiar with the wondrous wiles of the machine gun, and it is doubtful that he had ever recovered from the cry of "Kill, Kill!" with which the Army tries to shape its troops.

Torrio didn't have to urge Capone. The man who was to make a singular mark in the rackets set himself up in the Windy City almost immediately as:

> *Alphonse Capone*
> *Second Hand Furniture Dealer*
> *2220 South Wabash Avenue*

or, at least, so read his card.

Al Capone's job was to keep Torrio's competition under control through whatever means were necessary. The sawed-off shotgun, the well-timed police payoff, the intimidation of speak-easy owners, all were weapons in Capone's arsenal of terror.

It was only a matter of a few years before Al Capone had left his mentor far behind in the hierarchy of brutality. It was Capone, not Torrio, who threw over the rival organizations through an unparalleled campaign of wholesale murder. What the war hadn't taught him, the rackets had.

Capone's methods of eliminating his rivals weren't pretty, but they were effective. Sometimes the victim was "taken for a ride," a classic gangland procedure in which the unsuspecting was lured into a car, driven into the country and summarily murdered. Sometimes a car bearing a full complement of thugs would open fire on the passengers of another, slaughtering all before making a getaway. Sometimes a room would be rented within shooting distance of the "enemy," who was subsequently "nailed," in the argot of the times, with machine gun fire while entering or leaving his home.

The whole thing reached its apex on February 14, 1929 when, disguised as policemen, the Capone mob took care of the rival O'Banion contingent in the infamous St. Valentine's Day Massacre. All in all, the general public was largely immune to the nefarious goings-on. Yet more than 500 gangland murders occurred in the Chicago of the 1920s.

Like a kind of feudal baron, "Scarface Al" lived in an atmosphere of shaky popularity, issuing orders from his headquarters in the Hawthorne Hotel. When he traveled, it was in the style of a South American dictator, ensconced in an armored limousine flanked fore and aft by other limousines carrying members of Al's personal bodyguard.

As the 20s came to an end, Alphonse Capone was in control of an alcohol-based revenue which would make a Baptist tipsy. Recorded estimates state his income from $60 million to $100 million a year. He was known throughout the country, sometimes as a villain, all too frequently as a sort of hero. He controlled the sale of liquor in Chicago, and it is said the tentacles of his organization reached into such remote areas as Canada and Florida.

Arrested and imprisoned for 10 months in Philadelphia for carrying firearms, Capone was rarely so harassed. He rode the crest of the Prohibition wave, attending football games and theatres usually surrounded by a dozen or more well-dressed bodyguards.

When not in Chicago, he held forth in a splendid estate in Miami. He seemed above the law, almost idolized by a people who, for their own personal reasons—including, in all probability—annoyance with the lack of realism of the prohibition experiment—frequently glamorized its gangsters.

Defeat came to Capone after the 20s had met a violent death in the aftermath of the Wall Street Crash. In 1931, the master criminal was convicted and jailed for income tax evasion. It seems that Uncle Sam dislikes competition, too. Capone lived on for 16 years, dying in Florida after World War II had ended and the time which he made his own was only a memory.

TEXAS GUINAN

*"Where the hell would I be
without prohibition?"*
—Texas Guinan

Where indeed?
The "butter and egg man"—speakeasy euphemism for rich
man from out of town was just what Texas Guinan ordered.

A night club hostess, who greeted her guests with the
now-classic "Hello, Sucker!," could have been expected to
offend her clientele through such remarks. It was Miss
Guinan's special talent that through her wisecracking, often
at the expense of her patrons, she managed to leave them
laughing, often enchanted.

Instead of responding with indignation or annoyance, the big-time-spender from the Midwest, or upstate, or even the Manhattan suburbs, did just what Texas wanted him to do. He spent—and spent, often sums of money that were fantastic, even by today's standards.

Born Mary Louise Cecilia Guinan in Waco, Texas, and a veteran of the circus, vaudeville and some unspectacular western movies, Texas appeared in New York in 1922 at the age of 28. For the next decade, she hostessed a number of Manhattan Speaks with a salty gusto, always with one eye on the door to detect the intrusion of the long arm of the law.

When she was arrested, and that happened fairly frequently, the Big Girl from Waco seemed almost to enjoy herself. She knew how to handle the "Feds." She was never in jail, and simply being carted off toward one now and again struck her as something of a lark—just another incredible symptom of an incredible age.

A master of the art of "Y'all Come," she knew as did few others, how to squeeze blood out of a turnip—or a sucker. Although her prices were exorbitant, the suckers stood in line for the privilege of paying them. What Texas offered in return was homespun and simplistic, less than compelling talent with faint overtones of naughtiness.

Her wit may have been insulting, but, like an early Don Rickles, she kept her patrons coming back for more—as long as prohibition made the game worth playing.

Unlike Parker, Lewis, Fitzgerald and the rest, who lived well beyond the age that had made them as famous as they had made it, Texas Guinan died simultaneously with her era.

Where would she have been without prohibition? Nowhere. For once in history, life and death were not ironic.

HELEN MORGAN

*"(Helen Morgan is) a composite
of all the ruined women in the
world . . ."*
—James Montgomery Flagg

If Texas Guinan represented the spirit of fun and games,
1920s style, balance was provided by Miss Helen Morgan who
capitalized on sorrow. The original melancholy baby, she
went through her brief life with a sad song on her lips, a tear
in her eye and a hunger in her heart.

As her theme, this singer/nightclub proprietress beseechingly
sang "Why Was I Born?" There was more than irony in the
musical question, because it seems certain that she never
found out.

There are those who doubt that a white woman can
convincingly sing the blues. Few can or could. Helen Morgan,
in an increasingly sophisticated era that was losing its
fondness for vaudeville, found her metier in the middleground
of torch music.

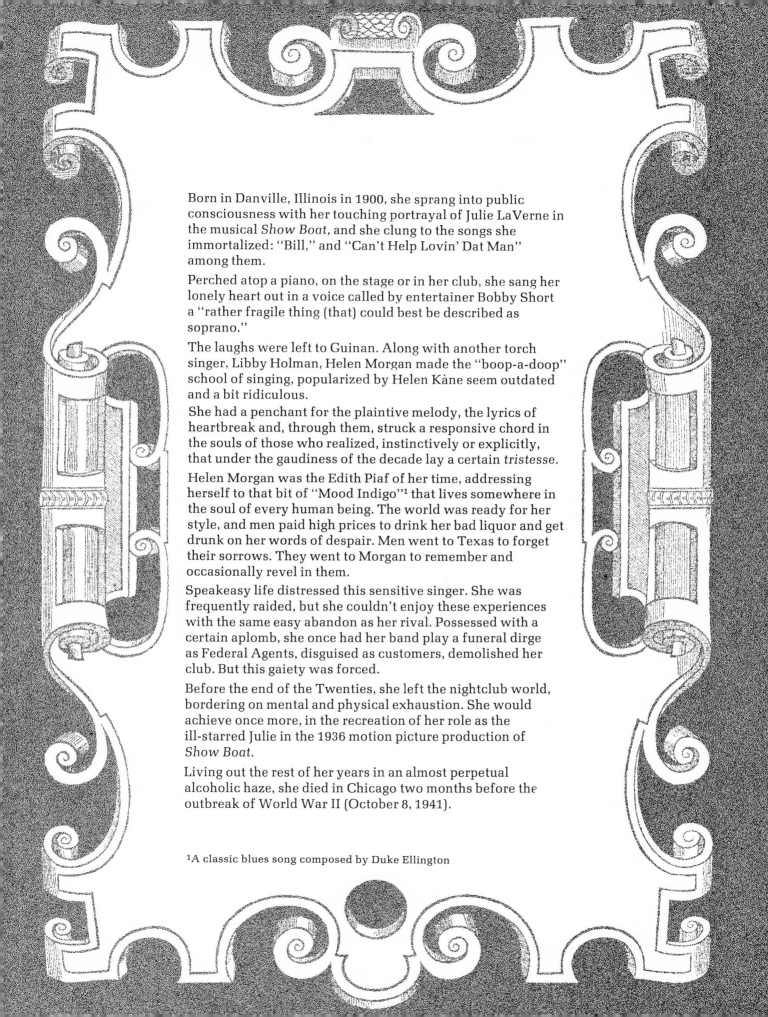

Born in Danville, Illinois in 1900, she sprang into public consciousness with her touching portrayal of Julie LaVerne in the musical *Show Boat,* and she clung to the songs she immortalized: "Bill," and "Can't Help Lovin' Dat Man" among them.

Perched atop a piano, on the stage or in her club, she sang her lonely heart out in a voice called by entertainer Bobby Short a "rather fragile thing (that) could best be described as soprano."

The laughs were left to Guinan. Along with another torch singer, Libby Holman, Helen Morgan made the "boop-a-doop" school of singing, popularized by Helen Kàne seem outdated and a bit ridiculous.

She had a penchant for the plaintive melody, the lyrics of heartbreak and, through them, struck a responsive chord in the souls of those who realized, instinctively or explicitly, that under the gaudiness of the decade lay a certain *tristesse.*

Helen Morgan was the Edith Piaf of her time, addressing herself to that bit of "Mood Indigo"[1] that lives somewhere in the soul of every human being. The world was ready for her style, and men paid high prices to drink her bad liquor and get drunk on her words of despair. Men went to Texas to forget their sorrows. They went to Morgan to remember and occasionally revel in them.

Speakeasy life distressed this sensitive singer. She was frequently raided, but she couldn't enjoy these experiences with the same easy abandon as her rival. Possessed with a certain aplomb, she once had her band play a funeral dirge as Federal Agents, disguised as customers, demolished her club. But this gaiety was forced.

Before the end of the Twenties, she left the nightclub world, bordering on mental and physical exhaustion. She would achieve once more, in the recreation of her role as the ill-starred Julie in the 1936 motion picture production of *Show Boat.*

Living out the rest of her years in an almost perpetual alcoholic haze, she died in Chicago two months before the outbreak of World War II (October 8, 1941).

[1]A classic blues song composed by Duke Ellington

CHAPTER EIGHT

*Those Who
Rebelled,*

*Those Who
Created*

Disenchantment has always furnished a fertile ground for the artist. Among the serious, disenchantment was the ruling emotion of the Twenties. Those who stopped to scrutinize the world around them saw it as a world without direction, without values, without meaning. This was the essence of the "Lost Generation."

The intellectuals and the talented tended to drift into their private enclaves in Greenwich Village, Chicago and Paris and there they remained throughout the decade or longer, free to speculate, debunk (as Mencken put it) and to produce.

Greenwich Village attracted the gifted in part because of its physical charm—picturesque and faintly European—and, in part, because of its low rents. Along with the brilliant Willa Cather, Theodore Dreiser, and the great Chicago writer, Sherwood Anderson, who deserted his midwestern roots for the East Coast, came, of course, the camp followers: those who believed that by adopting some of the eccentric ways of the talented they, too, would become talented. If sculptor Jo Davidson wore a beard—a rather unusual distinction in that day—suddenly everyone who fancied himself a sculptor had to wear one too. As with most imitators, the group which sprung up around the artists of the decade failed to realize that copying the peculiarities of the gifted does not, of itself, create a gift and that some accomplished artists have few peculiarities to imitate.

Poet-in-residence for the Village was Edna St. Vincent Millay; the Bible was a small literary review called "The Quill." The young flocked to the tea rooms which abounded in the area as today they converge upon the coffee houses. In the Village it has always been more fashionable to get drunk on ideas rather than on alcohol—even during Prohibition, a law of which few villagers approved.

The free-love, self-expressionistic side of the postwar Village, although it did exist, has largely been exaggerated. Most of those who gathered there came with seriousness of purpose. From the time of the celebrated 1913 Armory Art Show, which shocked the world with its deviation from conventionality, artists including John Sloan and Maurice Prendergast found in the Village's twisting streets a kind of intellectual harbor.

In Chicago gathered another impressive congregation, including for a time Theodore Dreiser and Sherwood Anderson, along with Carl Sandburg, Edgar Lee Masters and Vachel Lindsay. Anderson became famous with the publication of *Winesburg, Ohio* in 1919, and was to spend much of the next ten years in Paris at the courts of Gertrude Stein and Sylvia Beach. Masters published *The Golden Whales of California* in 1920 and went on to become the darling of the lecture set.

Ernest Hemingway was in Chicago for a time, and many critics believe that his style was greatly influenced by that of Sherwood Anderson. Anderson, who considered himself to be influenced by the writings of Gertrude Stein, believed he saw the touch of genius in the young Hemingway and it was he who wrote the young writer a letter of introduction to Miss Stein when Hemingway made his celebrated Hegira to Paris, thereby assuring him entree into that city's distinguished literary circle.

Brought about in part by the writings of Sinclair Lewis and H. L. Mencken, both of whom effected brilliant dissection of American society, appalled by the ordeal of Sacco and Vanzetti, dismayed with the realities of the Harding and Coolidge administrations, displeased with Prohibition and the disregard for law which it produced, many of America's writers were, in time, to find their way to Paris. That city loved its artists, even expatriate American artists, and did not attempt to interfere with the lives and spirits of the creative.

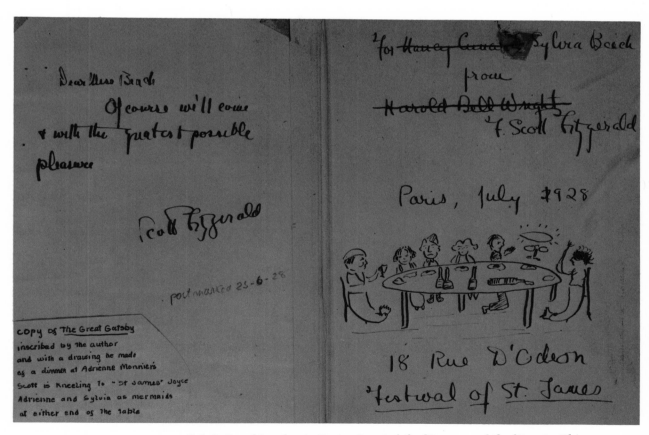

Sylvia Beach's salon in Paris attracted the literary and the literate. This inscribed copy of *The Great Gatsby* shows the whimsical affection of Scott Fitzgerald. The original is with the Beach papers. Firestone Library, Princeton University.

Sylvia Beach had proved that serious works could be published even if they did contain four-letter words, through bringing forth the American-banned works of James Joyce. Paris was humming with talent and the salons of Miss Beach and Gertrude Stein, along with her constant companion, Alice B. Toklas, brought together artists of every persuasion —from Virgil Thompson to F. Scott Fitzgerald to Pablo Picasso. These two ladies lived in Paris throughout most of their adult lives and provided a kind of catalyst between the French and the Americans. It is impossible to overemphasize their influence on American letters during the decade. They had found their homes in Paris, were eager to welcome other Americans to their new ways of life and new friends, and through entertainments and encouragement brought together writer with writer with painter with composer with performer, to the benefit of everyone involved. It often seemed that practically everyone with talent was involved.

The rue de l'Odeon, Paris, was a literary landmark. Owned by Sylvia Beach, it was a mecca for the English-speaking writers of the day.

Shortly after their marriage, novelist Sinclair Lewis and journalist Dorothy Thompson sailed for America. Two brilliant people, and one disastrous marriage.

At about this time Picasso was in his second rose period—which extended through 1927—and enjoyed associations with Braque and Guillaume Apollinaire. In Miss Stein's account of her enduring friendship with Picasso, she observed that the great artist thrived on friendships with writers which he preferred to friendships with fellow painters. Writers seemed to provide the stimulation he needed to go on with his work—he was and is a master of every medium of the visual arts. His superior talent did not require the conversation and opinions of other painters.

Shakespeare, Inc., the book store-publishing organization of Sylvia Beach, was a focal point in the lives of many of the American writers, and these writers were, amazingly enough, enormously popular with French readers. Their success with the discriminating French, who are as particular about the books they read as they are about the wines they drink and the foods they eat, was due, in large part to Adrienne Monnier, who translated numerous American works, often alone and sometimes in collaboration with Miss Beach.

It was she who made Walt Whitman known to France and who translated the writings of William Carlos Williams, Ernest Hemingway, and e.e. cummings. Considering the literary fecundity of the period, her achievement in compiling a catalogue of all American writing which had been translated into French (a task she had already performed with English literature) was considerable.

Sylvia Beach, a tough-minded but gentle person, was a great friend to Hemingway and to Scott Fitzgerald, who seemed to be losing his talent after publication of what is generally considered his best book, *The Great Gatsby,* in 1925. He had come to Paris in an effort to find it again. Fitzgerald was an admirer of James Joyce and it was Sylvia Beach who introduced them and who tactfully wrote that Scott's excessive drinking was merely an effort to spend all the money he was making.

Archibald MacLeish was another member of the coterie as was George Antheil, from Trenton, New Jersey, a gifted if highly controversial composer. In 1925, when his *Ballet Mecanique* was premiered, almost every member of this circle of incredible creativity attended, among them T. S. Eliot, James Joyce and Ezra Pound.

American composer and writer Virgil Thompson who, in 1926, changed from his original neoclassic, dissonant style to one of greater simplicity, was an integral part of the group. His music, performed today, is appreciated by most music lovers. In the Twenties he was considered to be a great radical, as was the late Igor Stravinsky, the student of Rimsky-Korsakov who made musical headlines with

Le Sacre du Printemps in 1913. In the Twenties he was to startle the world again with an opera-oratorio, *Oedipus Rex,* which featured a text by Jean Cocteau based upon the original by Sophocles.

For most of the serious painters, composers, writers, life in Paris was an invigorating, heady experience, rich in interaction between the various art forms and nationalities, feeding upon friendship, understanding and respect.

There is, however, a tragic footnote. One great American composer lived out the decade as he had for many years before, as a seller of insurance. It was not until 1939 that the magnificently inventive Charles Ives was discovered, along with the music he had created in every spare minute, year after solitary year. He was a composer in the manner of Schoenberg and Stravinsky, anticipating many of their ideas. During the Twenties he wrote to an empty house.
Nobody knew his name.

"The rich are different from you and me" observed Scott Fitzgerald, a novelist fascinated by beautiful people. In the 20's, the rich lived well by any standards.

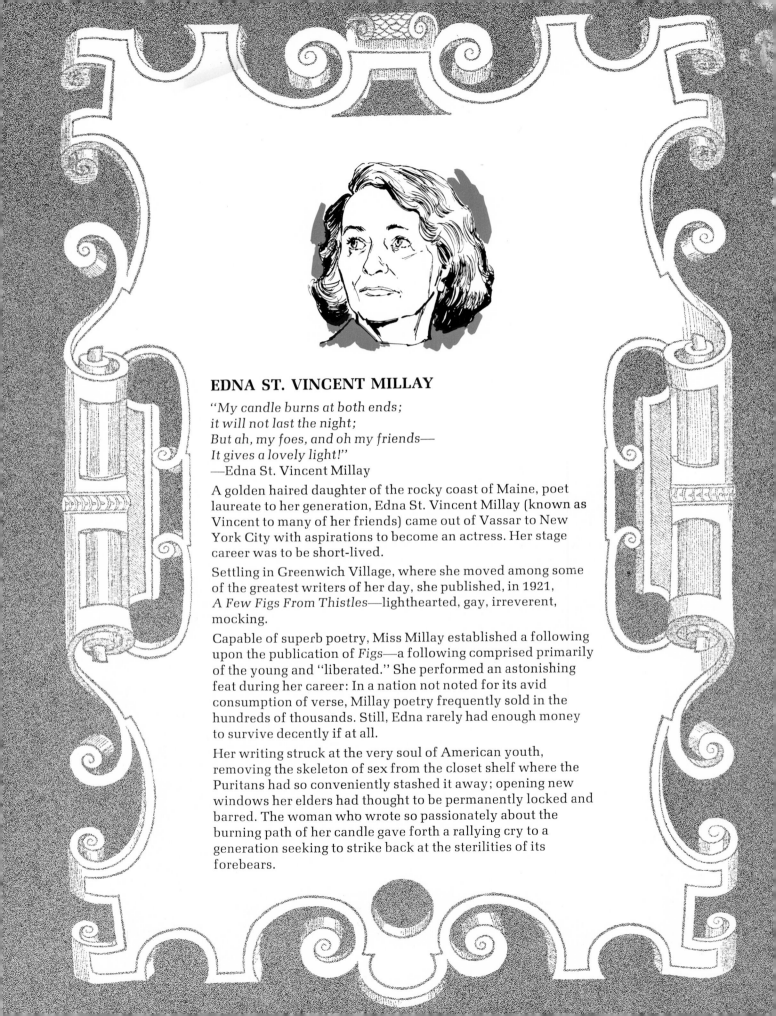

EDNA ST. VINCENT MILLAY

"My candle burns at both ends;
it will not last the night;
But ah, my foes, and oh my friends—
It gives a lovely light!"
—Edna St. Vincent Millay

A golden haired daughter of the rocky coast of Maine, poet laureate to her generation, Edna St. Vincent Millay (known as Vincent to many of her friends) came out of Vassar to New York City with aspirations to become an actress. Her stage career was to be short-lived.

Settling in Greenwich Village, where she moved among some of the greatest writers of her day, she published, in 1921, *A Few Figs From Thistles*—lighthearted, gay, irreverent, mocking.

Capable of superb poetry, Miss Millay established a following upon the publication of *Figs*—a following comprised primarily of the young and "liberated." She performed an astonishing feat during her career: In a nation not noted for its avid consumption of verse, Millay poetry frequently sold in the hundreds of thousands. Still, Edna rarely had enough money to survive decently if at all.

Her writing struck at the very soul of American youth, removing the skeleton of sex from the closet shelf where the Puritans had so conveniently stashed it away; opening new windows her elders had thought to be permanently locked and barred. The woman who wrote so passionately about the burning path of her candle gave forth a rallying cry to a generation seeking to strike back at the sterilities of its forebears.

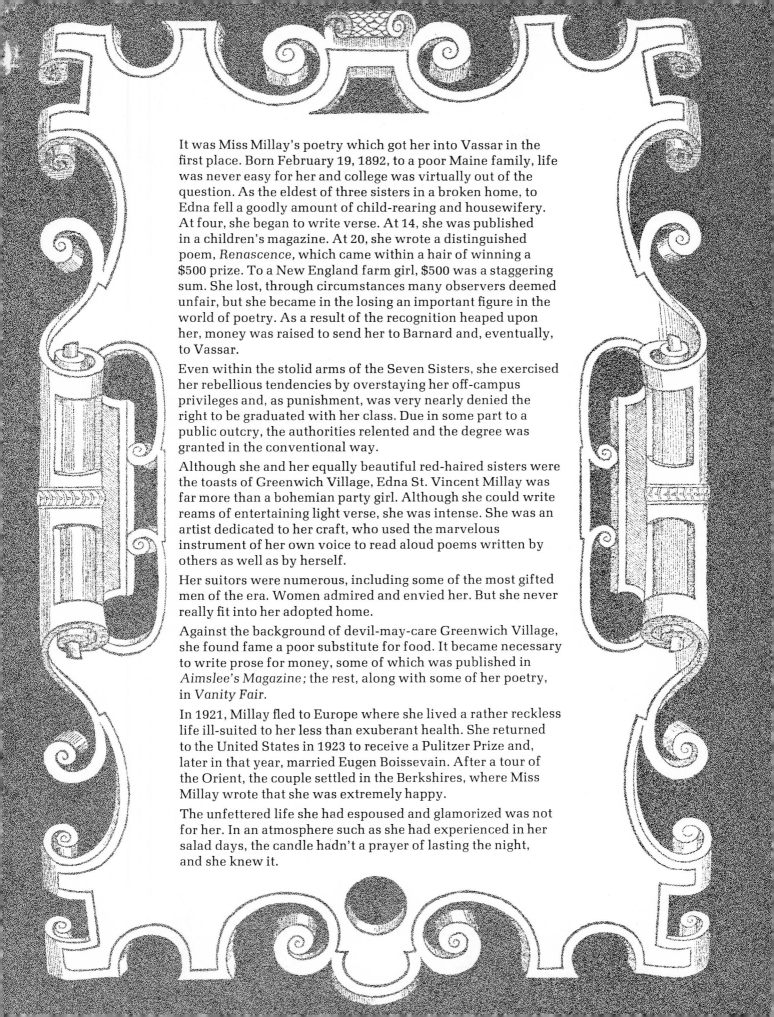

It was Miss Millay's poetry which got her into Vassar in the first place. Born February 19, 1892, to a poor Maine family, life was never easy for her and college was virtually out of the question. As the eldest of three sisters in a broken home, to Edna fell a goodly amount of child-rearing and housewifery. At four, she began to write verse. At 14, she was published in a children's magazine. At 20, she wrote a distinguished poem, *Renascence*, which came within a hair of winning a $500 prize. To a New England farm girl, $500 was a staggering sum. She lost, through circumstances many observers deemed unfair, but she became in the losing an important figure in the world of poetry. As a result of the recognition heaped upon her, money was raised to send her to Barnard and, eventually, to Vassar.

Even within the stolid arms of the Seven Sisters, she exercised her rebellious tendencies by overstaying her off-campus privileges and, as punishment, was very nearly denied the right to be graduated with her class. Due in some part to a public outcry, the authorities relented and the degree was granted in the conventional way.

Although she and her equally beautiful red-haired sisters were the toasts of Greenwich Village, Edna St. Vincent Millay was far more than a bohemian party girl. Although she could write reams of entertaining light verse, she was intense. She was an artist dedicated to her craft, who used the marvelous instrument of her own voice to read aloud poems written by others as well as by herself.

Her suitors were numerous, including some of the most gifted men of the era. Women admired and envied her. But she never really fit into her adopted home.

Against the background of devil-may-care Greenwich Village, she found fame a poor substitute for food. It became necessary to write prose for money, some of which was published in *Aimslee's Magazine;* the rest, along with some of her poetry, in *Vanity Fair.*

In 1921, Millay fled to Europe where she lived a rather reckless life ill-suited to her less than exuberant health. She returned to the United States in 1923 to receive a Pulitzer Prize and, later in that year, married Eugen Boissevain. After a tour of the Orient, the couple settled in the Berkshires, where Miss Millay wrote that she was extremely happy.

The unfettered life she had espoused and glamorized was not for her. In an atmosphere such as she had experienced in her salad days, the candle hadn't a prayer of lasting the night, and she knew it.

GERTRUDE STEIN

"A rose is a rose is a rose . . ."
—Gertrude Stein

A stout, intelligent woman, almost always accompanied by the lean and whimsical Alice B. Toklas, Gertrude Stein was both author and patron of the arts.

Along with Sylvia Beach, Miss Stein, who was born in a Pittsburgh suburb in 1874, was a prime mover in the literary world of Paris, a city in which she lived from 1902.
Interested in modern art as well as books and writers, she bought from and encouraged such painters as Picasso and Matisse.

A Radcliffe graduate who had at one time attended Johns Hopkins University as a pre-medical student, she had both a talent to write and a talent to attract. In her work she avoided conventional forms, espousing instead a "moments of consciousness" approach which at times made her writing difficult to understand.

Mlles. Stein and Toklas made their home in the Rue de Fleurs near the Luxembourg gardens and the greats of the time found the ladies fascinating not only because of Gertrude's acknowledged prowess as an author but also because of what Miss Beach called the "continual banter" between the two of them. Their remarks, she wrote, "were inseparable" yet "Alice had a great deal more finesse than Gertrude. And she was grown up: Gertrude was a child, something of an infant prodigy." Both women adored Spain and everything Spanish. Alice was a superior cook and the *Alice B. Toklas Cookbook* is among the masterpieces of culinary literature.

In the years before World War II, the two established their own publishing company, Plain Edition, which brought out several of Miss Stein's books: *Lucy Church Amiably* and *Four Saints In Three Acts,* a play which was accompanied by music by Virgil Thompson.

It was Gertrude Stein who coined the phrase "Lost Generation" to describe the expatriates who flocked to her salon in the Twenties—Anderson, Fitzgerald and Hemingway among them.

It is impossible to discuss Miss Stein without reference to Miss Toklas since their lives were inextricably woven together. Gertrude's most famous work, *The Autobiography of Alice B. Toklas,* was actually her own autobiography, written as though it were the work of Alice herself—a rather surrealistic arrangement.

Gertrude Stein died in 1946, having witnessed the liberation of her adopted homeland. Alice B. Toklas lived some 20 years longer—far beyond most of those who had shared the golden years in Paris.

ERNEST HEMINGWAY

*"What is moral is what you
feel good after and what is
immoral is what you feel bad
after."*
—Ernest Hemingway in
Death in the Afternoon

A giant of American letters, whose works will probably
prevail long after the writings of many of his contemporaries
have crumbled into the ashes and dust of irrelevance, Ernest
Hemingway was big in every sense of the word.

He could write stories of passion and adventure. He was a
capable and accurate reporter. But his work is timeless, not
only for his clipped sentences, his peerless dialogue, his
enviable verbal economy, his ability to see through to the core
of all he covered. These are virtues to which every journalist
aspires. Few master the written word as Hemingway did.
But he is classic because he addressed himself to the real
problems of the human experience, the great themes of life,
death, honor, courage, survival.

"Papa" Hemingway was a lover and a drinker of some stature, who took what he wanted from life and never flinched at paying the piper.

He was always at the center of the action—as an ambulance driver in France during World War I, with Gertrude Stein in the salons and cafes of postwar literary Paris, in the boudoirs of various ladies, in the jungles of Africa, on the battlefields of Spain.

Fisherman, hunter, seeker after violence, this man was one of the first war writers who opted not to glamorize the horrors of combat, but to tell it like it was.

Although Hemingway often minimized his talents as a reporter, he began his career on the Kansas City *Star* where he learned the principles of journalism from famed editor C. G. Wellington. His reportorial instincts never left him. After becoming a national institution for his books and stories, the challenge of the fray led him to cover World War II from the European front.

Hemingway was at the top of his creative powers in the Twenties, at a time when the public was more interested in books of the ilk of John Erskine's *The Private Life of Helen of Troy* than in Hemingway's *In Our Time,* a serious book published in 1924.

In 1926, with the publication of *The Sun Also Rises,* the masses, spoon-fed on the trivia of Bernarr MacFadden, and the intelligentsia who lapped up H. L. Mencken's lambast with the zeal of a starving kitten at a bowl of half and half, all discovered Lady Brett Ashley. And they discovered Hemingway.

The Sun Also Rises presaged *For Whom The Bell Tolls,* a story of the Spanish Civil War which indicated fascism in all its forms, *To Have and Have Not* is considered by some scholars to stress the collective good over the welfare of the individual. If this were, indeed, Hemingway's message, his own individuality was never sacrificed. One of his later works, *The Old Man and the Sea,* was a graphic description of one man, pitting himself and his belief in himself against the worst nature has to offer.

Hemingway, seriously ill, died by his own hand in 1961. Some seven years before, the virile and courageous author had received the Nobel Prize for Literature.

SYLVIA BEACH

*"I know, for my part, what
I owe to Scott Fitzgerald . . .
but what so many other writers
owe to each other, is Sylvia's
secret."*
—Andre Chamson, French
novelist and a Director of the
National Archives of France.

Americans in Paris can often spend years in the City of Light, reveling in its beauty, delighting in its cuisine and wines, without ever overcoming the feeling that, no matter how good their French, how passionate their love for the country and its people, they remain somehow on the outside. Usually the feeling is valid.

As at least one wag has put it, "The French have a talent for including you—out."

One American lady, Miss Sylvia Beach, who was born in Baltimore in 1887, managed to become an integral part of literary Paris. She was loved and respected by expatriates and natives alike, serving as a catalyst which united the writers of several cultures, to the benefit of all concerned.

Miss Beach first visited Paris in the early years of this century, and once having been exposed to it returned again and again, even living out some of the years of the Great War in her adopted land.

During the 20s and 30s, Sylvia Beach was the founding proprietor of Shakespeare & Co., a bookstore which was, in fact, not so much a shop as a meeting place for French, Irish, English and American authors.

First located at 8 Rue Dupretren on the Left Bank, Shakespeare and Miss Beach moved in 1922 to 12 Rue de l'Odeon, an address which has become synonymous with literary achievement. During the years between the two wars it was a kind of home away from home for the authors of the Lost Generation.

Sylvia Beach was far more than a bookseller. As a publisher, she will always be remembered for her daring in printing James Joyce's *Ulysses*—a book long to be banned in the United States and England. She was, later, to publish several other books by that Irish genius.

Those who clustered around Miss Beach read like a *Who's Who of belles lettres* of the period: Ezra Pound, Gertrude Stein, Ernest Hemingway, Archibald MacLeish, Marianne Moore, D. H. Lawrence, Ford Maddox Ford, Steven Spender —among many others. Almost all inscribed first editions of their often-banned and now respected books to Sylvia.

George Antheil, a Trenton, New Jersey composer who came to Paris with the reputation of the "Bad Boy" of serious music, was received with welcome understanding by Miss Beach— who by no means restricted her sympathies to writers alone.

She was a friend of the talented, who took her role as prophet of the Twenties seriously, all the while not falling into the trap of taking *herself* too seriously.

Memoirs of those who crossed her literary path indicate that she was honored and beloved in the now-distinguished circle in which she moved.

Although her home was Paris for more than 40 years, the ashes of this wise and tolerant human being are interred in her family's plot at the cemetery in Princeton, New Jersey.

Upon her death in 1962, it was said that Sylvia Beach had made a singular contribution to the task she had set for herself: bringing writer together with writer and bringing the public closer to that craft which she most admired.

SINCLAIR LEWIS AND DOROTHY THOMPSON

"It was not only the unsparing unapologetic ugliness and the rigid straightness which overwhelmed her. It was the planlessness, the flimsy temporariness of the buildings, their faded unpleasant colors."
—Sinclair Lewis in *Main Street*

Babbitt and Main Street still exist, but not so ubiquitously as in 1920 when Sinclair Lewis made his trapped heroine, Carol Kennicott, into a household word.

Lewis was one of the first to show the prim and narrowminded the error of their ways and, for his efforts, he was to be the first American to receive the Nobel Prize in Literature.

It is a long journey from Sauk Center, Minnesota, where Lewis was born, to Yale, which more or less ignored him, to Stockholm.

Lewis made it.

Along his alcohol-riddled way, Lewis was married first to Grace Hegger, but the marriage was virtually at an end in 1927 when the novelist met the beautiful and perceptive Dorothy Thompson, a journalist of high order who was reporting from Europe for the Curtis Publishing Company.

Dorothy's home base was Berlin, and it was there that Sinclair Lewis met and won her. He proposed the moment he saw her and for months repeated the proposal wherever he happened to be. Speaking before a luncheon group, it is said that "Red," as his friends called him (although women tended to call him "Hal") stepped up to the lectern, queried "Dorothy, will you marry me?" and sat down. It was a kind of tribute difficult to ignore.

Sinclair Lewis was a man who had to make it with his mind. His face was marred and marked by a skin disease which, unlike adolescent acne, was only to grow worse as he grew older. He was sunken-chested, blessed with features that could not have been made beautiful had they been coated with magnolia petals. Still he held a curious attraction for women.

Dorothy Thompson, at the time of their meeting recovering from a shattering divorce, had everything going for her: incisive intelligence, journalistic ability, good looks and a stable personality.

She had reservations about marrying Lewis, reservations which she might have heeded. Yet as soon as the novelist's divorce was final, he and Dorothy were married in the Savoy Chapel, London.

The two had not a prayer of surviving as a unit.

Red encouraged Dorothy's career, then avowed that she was eclipsing him. She was not. A journalist and not a novelist, devoted to her husband, she understood thoroughly that she could not compete with him even if she chose to do so. There were happy moments—usually brought about by Dorothy's continued effort—but the marriage was doomed. Lewis, in his alcoholic anguish, was unable to maintain the relationship and his wife, in spite of her considerable inner resources, could not carry the marriage alone.

As their intimacy deteriorated, she became an international figure through her knowledge of, and repeated warnings about, the intentions of the Third Reich.

Lewis, still writing and still drinking, died in 1951. Dorothy Thompson outlived him by a decade.

FRANCIS SCOTT KEY FITZGERALD AND ZELDA SAYRE

"It was an age of miracles, it was an age of art, it was an age of excess, and it was an age of satire."
—Scott Fitzgerald

That they loved each other is a truism. That they destroyed each other is still open to discussion. But they lived together throughout their years of greatest happiness and ultimate despair.

Handsome, talented Scott Fitzgerald of St. Paul, Minnesota, and beautiful, accomplished Zelda Sayre, a Montgomery, Alabama belle, seemed made for each other.

They were married in 1920, he the gifted and tormented author, and she the cloistered girl looking for broader horizons. They had no way of knowing that their fond closeness would be tempered with unending battles—that Zelda would end the decade with an uncompromisingly zealous effort to become a dancer and, later, a writer—that Scott would live to see his talents eroded by drinking.

They had youth, good looks, ability, and they had competitive drives which were too much for the pair who "loved not wisely but too well." Their deaths and lives stand as monuments to the excesses of the Twenties.

No one outlined the era as poignantly as did Scott who made his mark early with the publication of *This Side of Paradise*.

No one enjoyed the new freedoms more than these two, as they cavorted in fountains, passed out at the parties of their tolerant friends, crossed and re-crossed the Atlantic with jet-set determination—all the while loving a lot, and crying too.

For many, the Fitzgeralds symbolized the Jazz Age—the phrase itself came from the title of a book Scott prepared with artist John Held, Jr.

They lived hard and if Scott, who had been reasonably temperate during his undergraduate years at Princeton, should drink too much to write it didn't really matter as long as the money lasted. The trouble was that the money did not last, and never was enough.

Scott and Zelda were married in New York's St. Patrick's Cathedral, full of hope, promise and joy. They were to find that the madcap escapades for which they were famous were not the answer. In time, with Zelda pregnant with their only daughter, Scottie, they realized that even the relaxation of the suburbs to which they had retreated was not the Utopia they sought. They turned to Scott's home town where the author was able to overcome his hedonism to write *The Beautiful and the Damned in 1922*.

Then it was back to the East and the party circuit once again. During this period Scott produced his finest work, *The Great Gatsby*, a story of life among the bootleggers. Next it was Europe, where Scott became friends with some talented contemporaries—Gertrude Stein and Ernest Hemingway among them. During the last part of the decade, he attempted to scale the ramparts of Hollywood, and it was in Hollywood that he was to die in 1940 while at work on his final novel, *The Last Tycoon*.

In 1930, the lovely Zelda suffered her first emotional collapse, and she was never fully to recover. Her novel *Save Me The Waltz*, not at all a bad book, was written in a hospital. It was in a fire in a sanitarium at Asheville, North Carolina that she finally died in 1948.

It is a pity that Scott Fitzgerald lived out his lonely days believing himself a failure. Upon his death Dorothy Parker commented "The poor son of a bitch"—a sentiment shared by many.

Scott Fitzgerald was not a failure. Today he is remembered as the crowning glory of the age he named, and he has become a sort of national institution. It is almost a sacred ritual to write of Scott Fitzgerald.

He was a man of his times—and Zelda a woman of them. And the times did not defeat them totally, for who could ever forget them?

ERICH MARIA REMARQUE

*"We are forlorn like children,
and experienced like old men,
we are crude and sorrowful
and superficial—I believe we
are lost."*
—Erich Maria Remarque in
All's Quiet on the Western Front

One of the most sensitive of the war writers, whose ranks included Ernest Hemingway and John Dos Passos, was Erich Maria Remarque, whose *All's Quiet on the Western Front* appeared in 1929. The German-born author told the story of war as it actually happened, a story of filth and misery and despair, as did Hemingway in *A Farewell to Arms* which was published in the same year.

H.L. Mencken was to call Remarque's work the best of all the books on World War I, and many critics agreed with him. Terse in style, yet warmly compassionate to the plight of the fighting man, *All's Quiet . . .* richly deserves its place among the classics of world literature.

It was destined to become a superior film, and to earn the scorn and condemnation of the war-glorifying Nazis as unpatriotic. When the movie was played in Berlin during the early 30s, Nazi gangs demonstrated, and riots in the streets occurred. Eventually the Third Reich banned both book and movie.

Born in 1898 in Westphalia, descended from a family which had come to the Rhineland after the French Revolution, Remarque was a handsome, soft-spoken man who avoided publicity and who was happiest in the company of good friends.

During the War, into which Remarque was drafted at the age of 18, he was wounded five times and, appropriately enough, served on the Western Front. In fact his famous title was derived from a phrase that frequently appeared in the Kaiser's communiques.

Other books followed the initial triumph, among them *The Road Back* in 1931, *Three Comrades* in 1937, *Flotsam* in 1941, *Arch of Triumph* in 1946.

In 1939, Remarque came to the United States and, subsequently, became a naturalized American citizen. He lost all feeling of being German—indeed he said that he talked, dreamed and swore in English. His later years were divided between America and Switzerland. Several more books were written, but none received the same unanimous acclaim that met the first. Most, however, were moving and well written.

Twice married to the former Ilsa Jeanne Zamboui, Remarque married actress Paulette Goddard, one-time wife of actor Charlie Chaplin, in 1958. The union endured until the author's death in the autumn of 1970. He was a gentle man and a teller of tales. His message was peace.

JEROME DAVID KERN

"We have not even the consolation of knowing that his work was done . . . Kern was 60, which means he had easily a score of years of his music to write. Now we shall never hear it."
—Deems Taylor, at the time of Jerome Kern's death.

If it had not been for Jerome Kern's habit of staying up late and, consequently, oversleeping in the morning, the music world would have been deprived of one of its great talents. It was morning sleepiness that caused him literally to miss the boat to London in 1915. The ship was the Lusitania and the voyage was to be her last.

The score for *Show Boat* would have been enough to ensure Kern's place in the history of the American musical theatre. The fact is that he wrote much more, contributing scores to plays and movies, writing the songs that were to become "standards," the songs one still hears on radio, television, in nightclubs and smoke-tinged bistros.

Jerry Kern was born into a comfortable and reasonably prosperous family. His mother, always interested in music, began his piano training in the composer's earliest years. As the boy grew up in New York and Newark he began to realize that music was his life. His father, naturally enough, wanted his son to follow his footsteps in the business world. Young Jerome, however, knew what he wanted, was active in school musical activities and pursued his muse.

After studies at the New York College of Music, Kern first tried to make himself known to Tin Pan Alley in 1904. Soon he had a hit, "How'd You Like to Spoon With Me?" and, from then on, he trained his sights to Shubert Alley—Broadway. In 1912 he did his first complete score, for *The Red Petticoat*. After that followed *Sally* in 1920, with its memorable "Look for the Silver Lining," and *Sunny* in 1925, which produced the memorable song, "Who?" Both were vehicles for Ziegfeld's Marilyn Miller.

Over the years, Kern collaborated with accomplished lyricists P.G. Wodehouse, Otto Harbach and Oscar Hammerstein II. This last was one of the most successful combinations in songwriting history. Each believed in a close relationship between a musical score and the other elements of a play, and each knew how to bring about that phenomenon. The influence of their work together has carried over to this day.

After the early 30s, Kern wrote only one play for Broadway— *Very Warm For May*—a flop which left in its wake the enchanting "All The Things You Are" which ranks along with "Smoke Gets In Your Eyes," "They Didn't Believe Me" and "The Song Is You" as one of Kern's masterpieces.

He had a special freshness which he brought to his composing that makes his music as charming today as it was when it was written. There is hardly a composer or performer in the world who does not respect, if not revere, the contributions of Jerome Kern.

His last score was for *Centennial Summer* in 1945, after which he departed Hollywood for New York to write the music for Broadway's *Annie Get Your Gun*. Five days later, Kern died of a heart attack. Irving Berlin, another monumental musical figure of the 20s, was called in to do the score—which he did well.

Married in 1910 to Eva Leale, also a musician, Jerome Kern enjoyed a happy relationship with her throughout a life which was by no means one dimensional. In spite of his sense of humor, his late hours, and his talent, he found time to put together one of the most notable private book collections of all time—a staggering assortment of first editions, manuscripts, letters and drawings. The cost of the catalogue alone was $6—in 1929.

It is said that the whole world mourned the death of this man, and it may be true. It is certain that those who knew him loved him and that those who are committed to the best in popular music are forever in his debt.

As a child, Jerome Kern confided to his mother that he would much prefer to be a *good* song writer than a successful one. He was both.

LANGSTON HUGHES

Langston Hughes was one of the first black Americans to make white Americans think at all about the Negro, except perhaps as servant or, sometimes, entertainer.

Edna Ferber cautiously pointed up the problem of bigotry through the octoroon, Julie, tragic heroine of the book and musical *Show Boat*. But she wrote from the point of view of the sympathetic white woman.

Langston Hughes wrote as a perceptive, deeply concerned, black man who refused to be victimized. Born in 1902, the gifted poet turned his back on accommodation as a means of survival in a menacing white world.

As he put it, "We younger Negro artists who create now intend to express our individual dark-skinned selves without fear or shame. If white people are pleased we are glad. If they are not, it doesn't matter. We know we are beautiful."

At one time a busboy in a Washington Hotel, where he came to the attention of poet Vachel Lindsay, Hughes attended Columbia University in Manhattan and, while there, discovered the multi-faceted world that was Harlem in the Twenties.

It was in Harlem that he came to know other outstanding blacks of the day and fell into the vanguard of the "Negro Renaissance." The black world was dependent on the good will of the white population, as it was to remain for some time. Yet its talent survived in the persons of such artists as Louis Armstrong, Paul Robeson, Josephine Baker, Aaron Douglas.

In a manner sensitive as a nocturne, Langston Hughes spoke for and of his race in a day in which it was neither fashionable, nor particularly prudent, to do so.

Hughes, who took some fairly giant steps in the raucous, flaming Twenties—made the path a little smoother for all of those who followed.

He was a rebel with a noble cause who, unlike the late Dr. Martin Luther King, lived long enough to see at least a part of his dream fulfilled.

JOHN RODERIGO DOS PASSOS

*"I've got to a point where I
don't give a damn what happens
to me: I don't care if I'm shot
or live to be eighty; I'm sick
of being ordered around."*
—John Dos Passos in *Three Soldiers*

Along with Hemingway and Remarque, John Dos Passos, a
Chicago-born Harvard graduate, deplored the war—in print.
Three Soldiers, a novel published in 1921, underlined
Dos Passos's concept, widely shared, that war is hell.
Indeed, is glory worth the price? Dos Passos thought not.

Socially aware, disillusioned with many of the values
flourishing around him, Dos Passos went on to write
Manhattan Transfer in 1925, a book in which he described the
empty existence of the typical New Yorker. War was not the
only issue which burned his consciousness.

U.S.A., published in 1937, was a trilogy including *The 42nd Parallel, 1919* and *The Big Money*. The three books explored America's first thirty years in the 20th century by bringing narrative, newspaper and magazine quotations and biographies of prominent persons. Dos Passos had evolved an unusual and provocative technique.

As a young man, John Dos Passos was considered something of a radical, but in later years he reversed himself on many of the issues. His second trilogy, *District of Columbia,* 1952, shows clearly his increasing conservatism.

His Hegira to the right was a slow one, beginning in the 30s— a poverty-stricken era in which there was no longer room for Fitzgerald's privileged characters and which caused Lewis, Hemingway and others to address themselves to the evils of fascism. Dos Passos was far from fascist, but his personality and style were in transition. He responded to the dilemmas of the decade in different fashion from his literary colleagues.

Many critics believe that his early work was his best, but few dispute the value of *Midcentury,* which appeared in 1961. A careful dissection of the contradictions and pitfalls of contemporary culture, it confirmed Dos Passos's place in the history of letters and assured the skeptics that analysis of the scene can come from right as well as left.

CHAPTER NINE

The Vicious Circle

*"Just a bunch of loudmouths
showing off, saving their
gags for days, waiting for a
chance to spring them."*
—Dorothy Parker

They met each day for lunch, at first in the Rose Room of Manhattan's Algonquin Hotel and, later, at a large round table in the Oak Room, reserved for them by the Algonquin's owner, Frank Chase.

Known first as the "Vicious Circle"—a name which many of them preferred—they were, in time, characterized as "Knights of the Round Table" by cartoonist Edmund Duffy. The sobriquet endured.

The group of writers and actors expanded from a small nucleus. In the beginning there were only Dorothy Parker, Robert Benchley and Robert Sherwood, all of whom were working together on the sparkling Vanity Fair magazine. Soon their numbers included the most witty, articulate and urbane collection of personalities ever to gather together in one place—except, as John Kennedy once put it, " when Thomas Jefferson dined alone."

The Algonquin was the seat of this lively company for two principal reasons: its proximity to the offices of *Vanity Fair*, and the warmth and welcome of innkeeper Chase who in later years extolled these talented persons in his own well-written and well-received memoirs.

From the original triumvirate, the Table was expanded to include Franklin P. Adams, columnist for the New York *World,* who boosted the fortunes of the Round Tablers by including their *bon mots*, complete with proper attribution, in his column; critic Alexander Woollcott, a beautifully spoken if rotund gentleman; satirical playwright George S. Kaufman; crusading columnist Heywood Broun, and other dazzling personalities.

Harold Ross, founder of the *New Yorker* magazine, was a regular and, although he talked little, in the prospectus for the publication, he reflected the mood of the talented company of which he was a part:

> "Its (the *New Yorker's*) general tenor will be one of
> gaiety, wit and satire, but it will be more than a jester.
> It will not be what is commonly called radical or
> highbrow. It will be what is commonly called
> sophisticated, in that it will assume a reasonable
> degree of enlightenment on the part of its readers.
> It will hate bunk."

Such was the spirit of the Round Table, a spirit, it was assumed, not shared by the "little old lady in Duluth."

All of the regulars were young and, by the end of the decade, each had made his intellectual and/or humorous mark upon the American scene.

The *New Yorker*—bankrolled in part by Ross's poker winnings at the Thanatopsis Pleasure and Inside Straight Club, a men-only auxiliary to the Round Table which met upstairs at the Algonquin on Saturday afternoons—became stunningly successful as we shall see. George Kaufman, sometimes in collaboration with fellow Round Tablers Marc Connelly and Edna Ferber, managed to light up the Great White Way on numerous occasions. There has rarely been a drama critic *cum* humorist of greater depth than Robert Benchley.

But quite apart from their individual accomplishments, many of them significant, these people are best remembered for their intelligence, their incisive styles, their skills with the verbal rapier, their hatred of "bunk."

Together, they traded insults and ideas, and matched their wit and wisdom with lighthearted, but trenchant, fervor. Because of who sat there, what they said, thought and created, the Round Table became an institution which, nearly 50 years later, can still excite the most placid imagination.

Some samples:

FRANKLIN P. ADAMS:

Upon viewing Helen Hayes's performance in *Caesar and Cleopatra*, F. P. Adams, known to all as F. P. A., observed that Miss Hayes was afflicted with "fallen archness." Other Adams immortalities:

"The trouble with this country is that there are too many politicians who believe, with a conviction based on experience, that you can fool all of the people all of the time."

"One notion of an optimist is a man who, knowing that each year was worse than the preceding, thinks next year will be better. And a pessimist is a man who knows the next year can't be any worse than the last one."

"Speaking of screen stars, there's the mosquito."

"Mr. Bernard Shaw says that school teachers ought to have babies. Well, he ought to know; he's had enough school teachers."

Intolerant of bores, Adams once saw a master of the uninteresting headed his way. Taking his hand, F. P. A. said "How are you that's fine" before leaving the unhappy young man alone and bemused.

ROBERT BENCHLEY:

"The biggest obstacle to professional writing is the necessity for changing a typewriter ribbon."

"In America there are two classes of travel first class and with children."

To a woman who had attempted suicide, "You want to go easy on this suicide stuff. First thing you know, you'll ruin your health."

"My college education was no haphazard affair. My courses were selected with a very definite aim in view, with a serious purpose in mind—no classes before eleven in the morning or after two-thirty in the afternoon, and nothing on Saturday at all. On that rock was my education built." (One wonders when he took lunch.)

"Anyone can do any amount of work, provided it isn't the work he is supposed to be doing."

DOROTHY PARKER:

"Excuse me, I have to go to the bathroom." (Pause.) "I really have to telephone but I'm too embarrassed to say so."

"Woman's life must be wrapped up in a man, and the cleverest woman on earth is the biggest fool with a man."

"A girl's best friend is her mutter."

Informed that a woman friend had broken a leg in England, Dorothy Parker rejoined "Probably sliding down a Barrister."

Asked for a sentence using the word "horticulture," Mrs. Parker responded instantly: "You can lead a whore to culture, but you can't make her think."

And, of her own poetry, not as negligible as she seemed to believe, "I was following in the exquisite footsteps of Miss Edna St. Vincent Millay, unhappily in my own horrible sneakers."

ALEXANDER WOOLLCOTT:

"A broker is a man who runs your fortune into a shoestring."

"You are married to a cuckold," Woollcott once announced to a woman luncheon guest.

On his friend, Michael Arlen, "Arlen, for all his reputation, is not a bounder. He is every other inch a gentleman."

The habitués of the Round Table found that they thrived on each other's humor, sparking their own repartee upon the talents of such capable adversaries. Despite caustic tongues —usually more vicious within the Inn-group than with the outside world—they somehow managed to remain friends.

Perhaps such a phenomenon could have survived only in an era as hysterical and irreverent as the Twenties. That these people not only existed, but managed to find each other and stay together, trading their barbs, criticisms, and observations on the culture, remains proof of one of the minor miracles of the decade—perhaps because the pungencies of their language masked an awareness of the world around them that all too few of their contemporaries were willing to admit, if they had any recognition at all.

The *New Yorker,* for instance, inspired a devotion on the part of its staff seldom paralleled in the editorial offices of any magazine.

There was fulmination about the gifted editor, Harold Ross. There was the dissatisfaction about his ways and moods, but there was also a realization that the publication was intended to be, and would remain, something special. It has.

Culled from the offices of the once chic *Vanity Fair,* from the table at the Algonquin, from any place where talent could be found and utilized, the staff at the *New Yorker* was as star-studded in the Twenties—and on into the Thirties, Forties and Fifties—as any weekly could hope to be. Of the original contributors to Ross's weekly, most have died: Thurber, Parker, Benchley, Woollcott. But the flavor of the magazine seems unchanged.

It is still not written for the "Little Old Lady" from Iowa; it is still unconventional; it is still a means for the reader to remain *au courant* about the changing city and the changing world.

If there is an increasing concern with internationalism, it is because America herself is more concerned. If the reviews are cogent and unremitting, it is the reflection of a New York reading public which refuses to be duped.

That this institution—and that is what it has become—was begun by a man as unpromising as Harold Ross appeared to be in his early days, is a part of its ongoing charm. Other periodicals seem to come and go, but the *New Yorker* just goes—onward and onward.

When poverty ended the decade, it did so with a vengeance. Here Heywood Broun, always (circle Broun) a crusader, helps dispense bread and coffee to the jobless.

HEYWOOD BROUN:

"A liberal is a man who leaves the room when the fight starts."

Of a Tallulah Bankhead play, "Don't look now, Tallulah, but your show's slipping."

"She leads away from aces and neglects to keep jump bids alive. But she is still my mother."

"I have known people to stop and buy an apple on the corner and then walk away as if they had solved the unemployment problem."

"Repartee is what you wish you'd said."

GEORGE S. KAUFMAN:

On Gertrude Lawrence's play, *Skylark:* "It was a bad play, saved by a bad performance."

"Satire is something that closes on Saturday night."

Commenting upon Charlie Chaplin's blood pressure, rumored to be down to 108, Kaufman queried, "Common or preferred?"

"In Boston, the test of a play is simple. If the play is bad the pigeons snarl at you as you walk across the Common."

After a dinner at the White House, Kaufman said to his hostess, "You have a good location, good food, and I'm sure the place should be a great success when it's noised around a bit."

"All Rochester must be in New York this week" commented Beatrice Kaufman, after encountering several hometown acquaintances on Fifth Avenue. "What a fine time to be in Rochester" countered her husband.

Many years later, in an anecdote which may be apocryphal, Kaufman was visiting Moss Hart, his sometime collaborator, at Hart's palatial estate in Bucks County, Pa. After being given a tour of the opulent house and grounds, Kaufman is said to have quipped: "Just think what God could have done if he had Moss's money.

DOROTHY PARKER

*"If I should labor through
    daylight and dark
Consecrate, valorous, serious,
    true,
Then on the world I may
    blazon my mark—
And what if I don't and what
    if I do?"*
—Dorothy Parker

Mistress of the *bon mot*, Princess Charming of the literary world that met for lunch at the famed Algonquin Round Table; critic, writer, poet and wit, Dorothy Rothschild Parker was led by the life she tried so desperately to lead.

Although her total literary output was small—two books of short stories, three books of poetry in addition to her essays and criticism—Dorothy Parker seemed to speak for her era and, perhaps, her personal confusion was only an extension of the confusion of her times.

She was born in 1893, to grow up in New York City under the firm discipline of her wealthy Jewish father and a conventional Roman Catholic stepmother. By the time she was 27, she was famous (her verse was first published in *Vogue* when she was 23) and her life stood as a reproach to the sensible manner in which she was reared. It was Dorothy's particular want to tear down the icons of society, to burp in the face of the ordinary, and this she did with a flair for the English language which threatens to make her immortal.

Alexander Woollcott, one of Mrs. Parker's Round Table compatriots, referred to her as a "combination of Little Nell and Lady Macbeth." Either description would, by itself, be misleading. Together they sum up the lady as only Woollcott could.

Bitchiness was Dorothy Parker's stock-in-trade, and she had mastered the art. Once, describing a guest at a party, Mrs. Parker was heard to say "That woman speaks eighteen languages and can't say 'No' in any of them."

When Mary Sherwood, wife of the well-known playwright, delivered a child (an event which Mrs. Sherwood had heralded at a bit greater length than Mrs. Parker thought appropriate) Dorothy cabled her forthwith: "Dear Mary, We all knew you had it in you." Through her blithe observations, DP was not above taking verbal swipes at the famous of the decade.

Upon learning of the death of Silent Calvin Coolidge, it was Dorothy Parker who casually inquired "How could they tell?" *Constant Reader,* the series of reviews which Mrs. Parker turned out for the *New Yorker,* contained her biting attack on A.A. Milne's *House at Pooh Corner:* "Tonstant Weader fwowed up."

As with most clowns, from the time of Pagliacci and before, Dorothy Parker's wit and irony were but camouflage for the reality of an aching, tortured soul.

In and out of prestigious beds—including, it is said, those of Hemingway, Lardner and Sherwood—and not much of a success at marriage, Dorothy Parker tried suicide on at least two occasions. These abortive attempts led to one of her better known poems:

> *"Guns aren't lawful;*
> *Nooses give;*
> *Gas smells awful;*
> *You might as well live."*

By the end of the 1920s, Dorothy Parker, who had long found drinking more appealing than eating, was beginning to degenerate into alcoholism. Writing, always difficult for her, was a vocation which she less and less pursued. Her attempts to conquer the theatrical world were disastrous failures. Although she knew a limited success in Hollywood, her efforts to make it as a screenwriter left her with a feeling of discontent.

She seemed to exist simply to play the role of Dorothy Parker, who had been called by some "the funniest woman in the world."

The humor had dissipated by that day in June (7), 1967, when a chambermaid found her dead in a dreary Manhattan hotel.

Dorothy Parker had died much earlier—probably with the decade for which she spoke.

ROBERT BENCHLEY

*"Abie's Irish Rose—America's
favorite comedy. God forbid."*
—Robert Benchley

In his lifelong fight against mediocrity, Robert Benchley was
not above making the American people feel mediocre
themselves if they fell for what he considered to be trash.
His running campaign against the Broadway show *Abie's
Irish Rose* became a symbol of all that this Harvard-educated
humorist considered to be inferior. As drama critic of the old
Life magazine (1920-1929) and later for The *New Yorker,*
Benchley was known for accurate, penetrating reportage as
well as for his feud with this publically popular play—a play
which seemed to go on and on forever, or so it appeared to
Benchley, his enemies and his friends. The play was an
artistic disaster and Benchley, recognizing a bad thing when
he saw it, used the show as a honing wheel for the two-edged
sword of his pen.

"*The Rotters* is no longer the worst play in town! *Abie's Irish Rose* has just opened," Benchley wrote. And throughout the five and one-half years of the run he also opined: "People laugh at this every night, which explains why democracy can never be a success." "Where do the people come from who keep this thing going? You don't see them out in the daytime." Toward the end of the run of the play, he put it more succinctly: "We don't like this play."

Literate and charming, this one-time junior editor of *Vanity Fair* and founding member of the Algonquin Round Table contributed scores of pieces to the magazines, combining his theatrical criticism with a fantastic output of gentle satire and sophisticated barb.

The Sacco-Vanzetti case horrified this conscientious man, who did not limit his caustic tongue to the Great White Way. It was he who obtained the testimony which bore witness to the anti-Italian inclinations of the presiding judge.

He was author of several excruciatingly funny books, including the celebrated *Chip Off the Old Benchley* and *Benchley Beside Himself,* and he was one of the few in the Vicious Circle who made it in the theatre, a goal toward which a good many of them aspired. Off Broadway he wrote short, ironic films in which he both acted and directed.

Despite his irreverence, it was Benchley who, at the end of the decade, announced that he was surfeited with sex as a stage dilemma. Some critics believe that this remark contributed to the demise of realism in the theatre, realism which had been sparked in the Twenties by the towering presence of Eugene O'Neill.

One of the most fecund talents of the era, Robert Benchley died in 1945, leaving behind a body of work which is still trenchant, still pertinent—and, perhaps most important, still read.

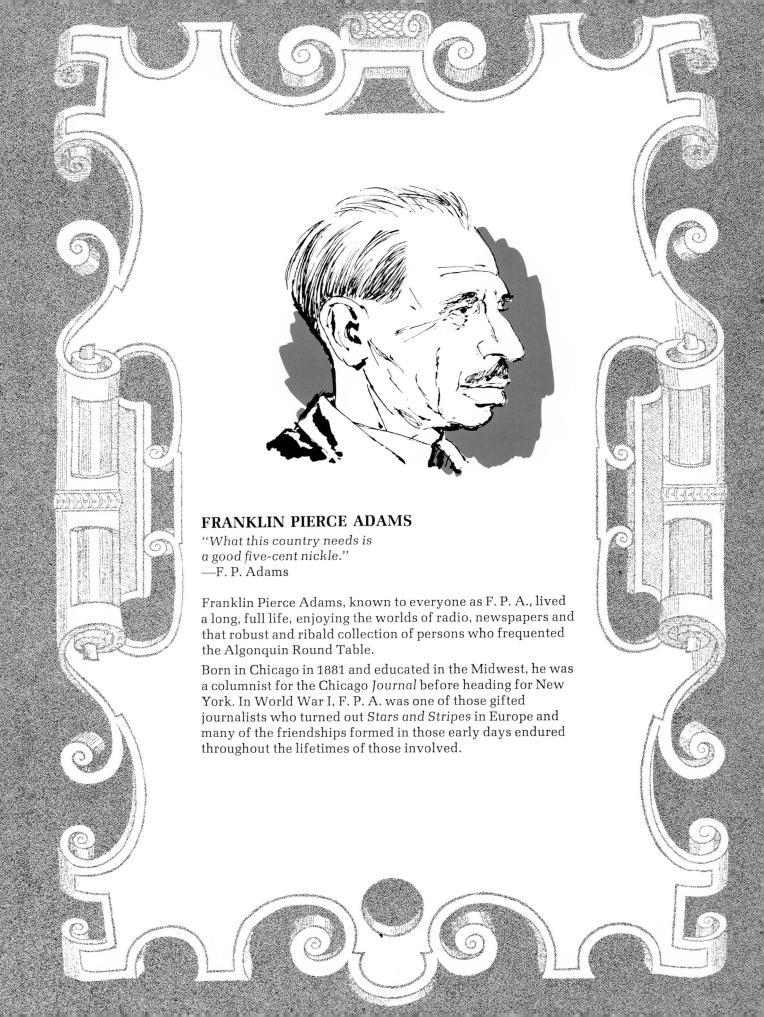

FRANKLIN PIERCE ADAMS

*"What this country needs is
a good five-cent nickle."*
—F. P. Adams

Franklin Pierce Adams, known to everyone as F. P. A., lived a long, full life, enjoying the worlds of radio, newspapers and that robust and ribald collection of persons who frequented the Algonquin Round Table.

Born in Chicago in 1881 and educated in the Midwest, he was a columnist for the Chicago *Journal* before heading for New York. In World War I, F. P. A. was one of those gifted journalists who turned out *Stars and Stripes* in Europe and many of the friendships formed in those early days endured throughout the lifetimes of those involved.

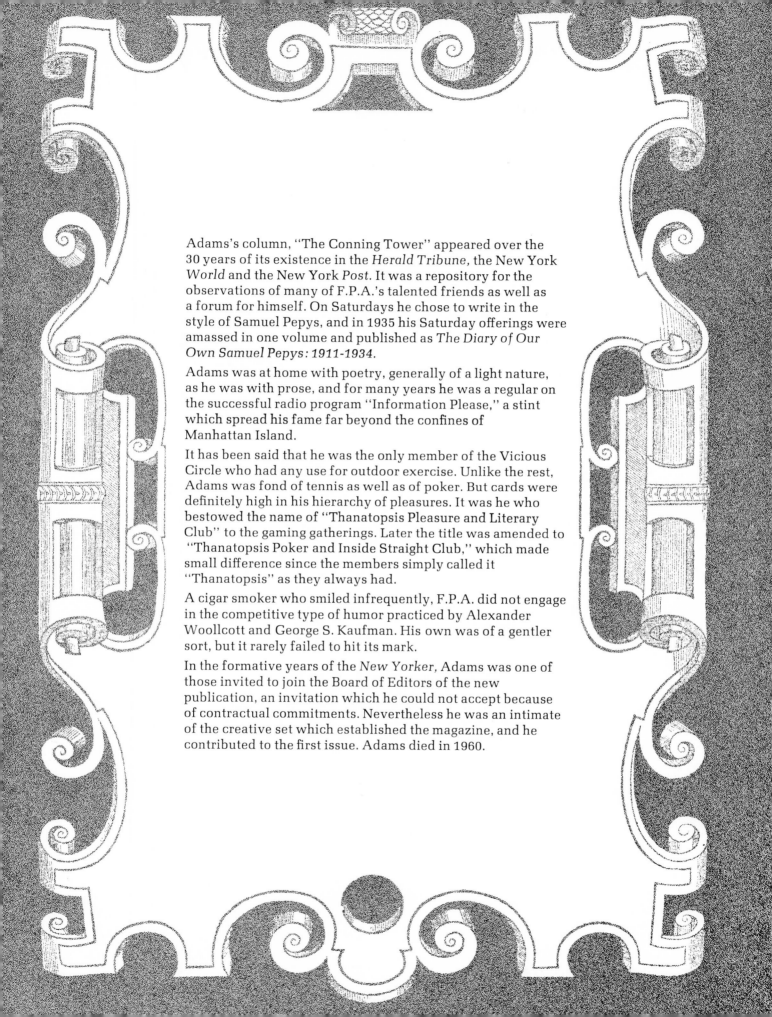

Adams's column, "The Conning Tower" appeared over the 30 years of its existence in the *Herald Tribune,* the New York *World* and the New York *Post.* It was a repository for the observations of many of F.P.A.'s talented friends as well as a forum for himself. On Saturdays he chose to write in the style of Samuel Pepys, and in 1935 his Saturday offerings were amassed in one volume and published as *The Diary of Our Own Samuel Pepys: 1911-1934.*

Adams was at home with poetry, generally of a light nature, as he was with prose, and for many years he was a regular on the successful radio program "Information Please," a stint which spread his fame far beyond the confines of Manhattan Island.

It has been said that he was the only member of the Vicious Circle who had any use for outdoor exercise. Unlike the rest, Adams was fond of tennis as well as of poker. But cards were definitely high in his hierarchy of pleasures. It was he who bestowed the name of "Thanatopsis Pleasure and Literary Club" to the gaming gatherings. Later the title was amended to "Thanatopsis Poker and Inside Straight Club," which made small difference since the members simply called it "Thanatopsis" as they always had.

A cigar smoker who smiled infrequently, F.P.A. did not engage in the competitive type of humor practiced by Alexander Woollcott and George S. Kaufman. His own was of a gentler sort, but it rarely failed to hit its mark.

In the formative years of the *New Yorker,* Adams was one of those invited to join the Board of Editors of the new publication, an invitation which he could not accept because of contractual commitments. Nevertheless he was an intimate of the creative set which established the magazine, and he contributed to the first issue. Adams died in 1960.

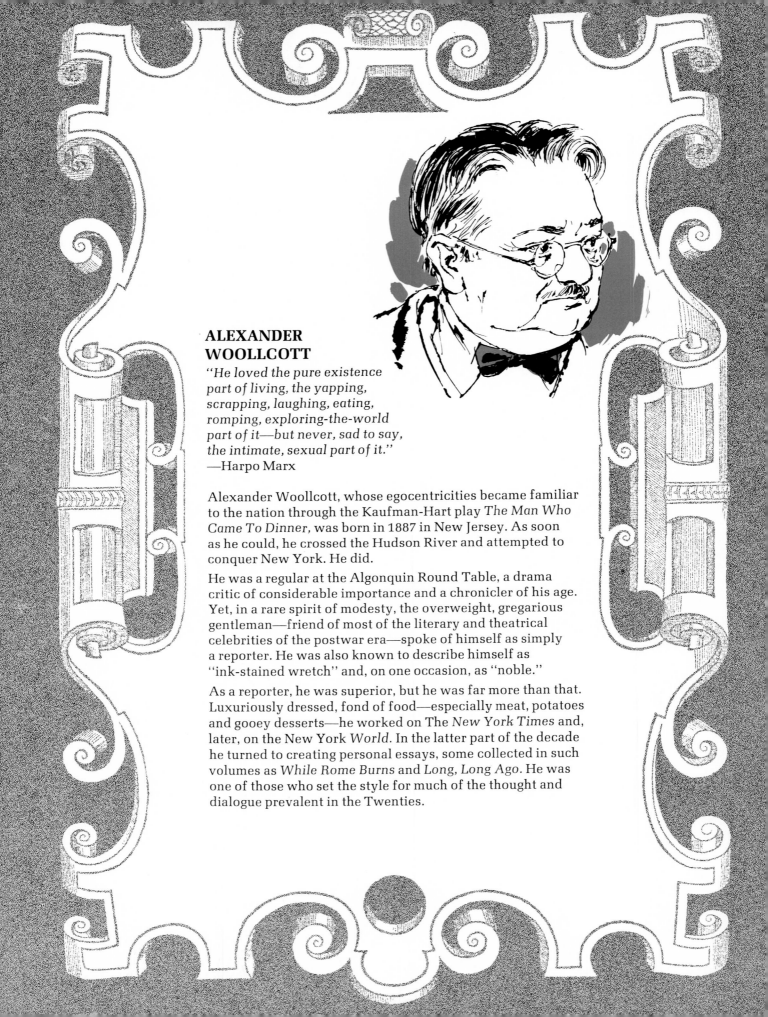

ALEXANDER WOOLLCOTT

"He loved the pure existence part of living, the yapping, scrapping, laughing, eating, romping, exploring-the-world part of it—but never, sad to say, the intimate, sexual part of it."
—Harpo Marx

Alexander Woollcott, whose egocentricities became familiar to the nation through the Kaufman-Hart play *The Man Who Came To Dinner*, was born in 1887 in New Jersey. As soon as he could, he crossed the Hudson River and attempted to conquer New York. He did.

He was a regular at the Algonquin Round Table, a drama critic of considerable importance and a chronicler of his age. Yet, in a rare spirit of modesty, the overweight, gregarious gentleman—friend of most of the literary and theatrical celebrities of the postwar era—spoke of himself as simply a reporter. He was also known to describe himself as "ink-stained wretch" and, on one occasion, as "noble."

As a reporter, he was superior, but he was far more than that. Luxuriously dressed, fond of food—especially meat, potatoes and gooey desserts—he worked on The *New York Times* and, later, on the New York *World*. In the latter part of the decade he turned to creating personal essays, some collected in such volumes as *While Rome Burns* and *Long, Long Ago*. He was one of those who set the style for much of the thought and dialogue prevalent in the Twenties.

During World War I he was a member of the staff of *Stars and Stripes,* a serviceman's newspaper of considerable merit. When not playing poker on the Place du Tertre, Montmartre, this gaggle of writers and editors turned out a really superior paper. The success is not at all surprising since those involved in the production included Harold Ross, Grantland Rice and F.P. Adams, not to mention Woollcott.

Sharp-tongued and occasionally nasty, Woollcott discouraged the non-productive from the Round Table by uttering such comments as "How are you today, Repulsive?" The weak willed ran for cover. George Kaufman, however, was Aleck's acerbic match, even though he worked for Woollcott on the *Times.* Apparently Kaufman was not afraid of losing his job because the verbal battles between the two were something to witness and their fellow Round Tablers enjoyed doing just that.

Several of Woollcott's friends—notably Harold Ross— delighted in misspelling his surname, a rather simple feat.

Aleck at times could prove to be a difficult friend to have. Very close to Ross and his first wife, Jane Grant, with whom he was eventually to feud, he lived with them at their apartment, 412 W. 47th Street. Aleck who, when annoyed with one or the other of a couple took macabre pleasure in driving married persons apart, is given credit by Miss Grant for causing some of the trouble which led to her divorce from Ross.

A bachelor until his death in 1943, Woollcott chaired a successful radio show, "The Town Crier" which, among other accomplishments, presented a spectacular birthday party for composer Jerome Kern in 1935.

James Thurber christened Aleck "Old Vitriol and Violets," and thus summed him up exactly. His mood often depended upon the food he was served and he could be worse than grumpy if the viands were disappointing.

Owlish and bespectacled, difficult and tempestuous, reckless and accomplished, he was a man talented enough to carry off his numerous idiosyncracies with relative aplomb. A lesser man should not try to copy him. There was only one Woollcott and he was inimitable.

HAROLD WALLACE ROSS

"Is Moby Dick the whale or the man?"
—Harold Ross

Unkempt, uncouth, less than well-educated, often clumsy, not well-spoken, Harold Ross seemed an unlikely candidate to create the magazine that has to this day remained synonymous with sophistication and worldliness. Yet the boy who was born in Aspen, Colorado in 1892, did it. And he did it well.

The *New Yorker* brought together a group of talents unparalleled in publishing history: James Thurber, Helen Hokinson, Alexander Woollcott, S. J. Perelman, Robert Benchley, Dorothy Parker, Peter Arno, E. B. White, and many, many more.

Ross was a superior editor who, himself, could not write at all—or so he said. He was fascinated by writers, but professed not to understand the creative process.

A hard worker, difficult to get on with, he ruled with the stick and largely forgot the lures of the carrot. He was a man so irascible as to be unapproachable at times. He demanded the best from the singularly gifted people whom he employed— and he almost always got it. He took the members of the Round Table out of the Algonquin, but he knew enough not to try to take the Algonquin spirit out of the Round Tablers. Recognizing and respecting talent when he saw it, Harold Ross made sure that the bright ideas of the Vicious Circle made the pages of his weekly and not just the conversations of the martini circuit.

He wasn't easy to work for, but he could draw forth enormous quantities of work from those around him. While his own literary tastes were far from well-developed, a kind of 6th or 7th sense made him a splendid judge of the best that the best had to offer.

He edited the *New Yorker* from 1925 until 1951—and it was so successful that, eventually, it was able to *reject* advertisements worth up to $1 million each quarter.

Profanity was a part of his speech and a part of his character, but it seemed to be a product of a cultivated inelegance and not rooted in some deeper sense of blasphemy. He was always restless, busy, pressed for time.

A loner, carefully protected by his secretary, Elsie Dick—a lady with the courage to sometimes overtly express dissatisfaction with Ross's mode and manner—he was little concerned with himself except that he, like Garbo, wanted to be alone. Both he and Miss Dick worked toward the continuation of his solitude.

James Thurber, a long-time worker in the *New Yorker's* champagne cellars, and later a faithful biographer of its editor, remarked upon Miss Dick's ability to steer Ross onto the elevator at the precise moment when the "coast was clear," thereby sparing him undesired meetings and conventional exchanges of pleasantries—an art at which Mr. Ross did not excel.

He began, as did so many, as a newspaperman, who during the last years of World War I edited the *Stars and Stripes* in Paris. And he began humbly: his first job was as a reporter for the *Salt Lake City Tribune* at the knowledgeable age of 14.

Always worried, harried, and, by his own admission, frequently harassed, Ross wanted the creative gifts of his brilliant staff utilized to the fullest. Yet he believed that the magazine should be run as a business and not as a salon. Wise and innocent, analytical and ignorant, direct to the point of rudeness, through his dedication and singleness of purpose, Harold Ross created a magazine which, 20 years after his death, is still a mainstay of the urbane and of those who wish to be.

EDNA FERBER

"Edna asked for no quarter . . . and she certainly didn't give any. In her home, she was an absolute monarch, who made Catherine the Great look like Little Orphan Annie."
—Bennett Cerf at Miss Ferber's funeral.

When Edna Ferber made it big in 1924 with *So Big*, which was to earn her a Pulitzer Prize the following year, she was 37 years old and had already written numerous books and plays. Everywhere one looked during the 20s and 30s, there was something on the market by Ferber. She was almost always successful and, from her earliest days, was never far from her typewriter.

A native of Kalamazoo, Michigan, who began her career at 17 as a newspaper reporter, Miss Ferber published her first book, *Dawn O'Hara* in 1911. She never married. Instead, she hobnobbed with the greatest wits of her time, including Alexander Woollcott and Noel Coward, and was often spotted at the Algonquin Round Table. She collaborated on several plays with acerbically amusing George S. Kaufman, and the money rolled in as the words poured out.

Everything Miss Ferber wrote saw the light of print, and she went one further. Nearly every book was destined for the best-seller list. She was a competent writer who worked at her craft, and was rewarded with honorary degrees from Adelphi College and Columbia University.

One of the major achievements of her long and distinguished career was the novel *Show Boat* (Chapter 12), a colorful indictment of racism which was to become one of the great Broadway musicals of all time and to appear on the motion picture screen in 1929, 1936 and 1953.

If she actually were the "absolute monarch" which Bennett Cerf was to call her after her death in 1968, she drove no one harder than herself. At 82, and ailing, she was at work on yet another book.

Hard work paid off for this woman. She accumulated a large estate and a bundle of gifts to literature and the theatre that, in the words of "Ole Man River," won't be soon forgotten.

A wit, a savant, a creative person among creative persons, she might have been called "Multi-Media Edna" if she were to be analyzed in the press of today.

Variety, that hardest to please of show business periodicals, opined after her death that Miss Ferber's plays and novels "provided motion pictures with such natural scenarios that many of them read as if written for the film medium."

That was probably not her intent. Edna Ferber wanted to be a good novelist, and she was—through a combination of perception, diligence and long life that eludes most of us. When Edna Ferber died, her work was still in demand— except from those Texas critics who disliked her book *Giant,* which didn't speak too fondly of their state.

From the point of view of nearly everyone else, Edna Ferber died long before she should have.

Vice President Calvin Coolidge was sworn into the highest office on August 3, 1923, in the Coolidge family farmhouse in Plymouth, Vermont.

In his initial statement to the country, Silent Cal, as he came to be known, averred "It will be my purpose to carry out the policies which he (Harding) has begun for the service of the American people and for meeting their responsibilities wherever they may arise." It is safe to assume that Mr. Coolidge had little knowledge of some of the less fortunate activities of the Harding administration.

When Warren G. Harding died in August, 1923, he was mourned throughout the country. He had made a mess of government, but few citizens realized that, yet. He had been duped—not once, but several times—by the offices he had headed with his friends.

Harding had taken particular pride in the work of Colonel Charles R. Forbes, whom he had installed as head of the Veterans Bureau. When the president became aware of the corruption in Forbes's office—corruption involving deals with the contractors who had been engaged to build veterans' hospitals, it was the first inkling the genial Mr. Harding had that anything was going wrong. His reaction was clear and certain astonishment: "That can't be." Nevertheless he instituted an investigation and, within a few days, he requested and received Forbes's resignation. Charles F. Cramer, legal adviser to the Veterans Bureau and

William Howard Taft (R) and Warren Harding (C) with Abraham Lincoln's son, Robert, at the dedication of the Lincoln Memorial in 1922.

close associate of Forbes, subsequently shot himself.

While the public reacted quietly, almost vaguely, to the corruption in the Bureau and the resignation and suicide that it prompted, Harding seemed to sense what it portended. The burdens of the Presidency, which he had taken fairly lightly, began to weigh heavily on his broad but inadequate shoulders. He was disillusioned and dismayed. It was dawning upon this kindly but unsophisticated man that his unquestioning loyalty to his friends, his trust in the fundamental goodness of human nature, could prove to be a virtue which would destroy himself—and his country.

Tired and despairing, he went to the people for relaxation and the stimulation of face to face contact with those he governed. Harding met people easily and spoke well. He had hoped to be revitalized; instead, it was to be his last trip.

On June 20, 1923, he left Washington. He was returned to the White House, dead, on August 7.

Coolidge was a conscientious man, lacking in color, fond of lengthy afternoon naps, but he did his duty as he saw it. When, in the months following Harding's death, the deficiencies of the administration were gradually uncovered, it is doubtful that anyone was more appalled than Calvin Coolidge. He had been aware that the Forbes operation had, in two years, milked the country of about $200 million. The chances are good that that was about all he knew.

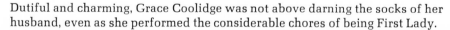

Dutiful and charming, Grace Coolidge was not above darning the socks of her husband, even as she performed the considerable chores of being First Lady.

Robert La Follette, the progressive Senator from Wisconsin seemed to think that the misdeeds of the government had not begun and ended with the activities of the Veterans Bureau. He urged a committee to investigate various government oil leases. Such a committee was set up under the chairmanship of Senator Thomas Walsh of Montana. The findings were shocking. With the authority of Warren G. Harding himself, Albert Fall, Secretary of the Interior, had leased government oil reserves which were ostensibly maintained for the use of the U.S. Navy to the Pan-American Petroleum Corporation, headed by Edward Doheny. It was also revealed that Fall had accepted $100,000 from the Doheny family in exchange for an unsecured note.

The Pan-American lease of the reserves at Elk Hills, California, paled before the next revelation: With the aid of the Secretary of the Interior, one Harry Sinclair had leased the oil reserves at Teapot Dome, Wyoming. The transaction took place without competitive bidding and, as compensation, Albert Fall's son had received more than $2 million in liberty bonds while Fall, himself, had walked away from the deal with something like $85,000 and a healthy herd of cattle. Not bad pay.

The whole arrangement had been highly improper. Why should the government have chosen to lease the land at all and, if it had chosen to do so, why had there been no public bidding? The answers were not forthcoming and eventually Albert Fall was fined $100,000 and sent to jail.

Teapot Dome might have remained in obscurity for a good many years had it not been for a letter from an unknown citizen of Wyoming who wrote his Congressman that these reserves had been leased by the Secretary of the Interior to Harry Sinclair through a corporation known, appropriately enough, as the Mammoth Oil Company. The letter writer was in the oil business himself, so he naturally had an interest in the affair. His Congressman, Senator John B. Kendrick, was a Democrat who took little delight in sweeping Republican bungling under the national rug. Such is the power of the pen.

Before it was all over, the scandals of the Harding years were to reach all the way to Attorney General Harry Daugherty himself, closest of Harding's personal friends and his long time mentor.

Thomas Miller, alien property custodian for Harding, had received $50,000 in bonds in return for selling valuable German chemical patents for a fraction of their real worth. The bonds were deposited in Daugherty's account in the Daugherty family bank in Washington Court House, Ohio. In an unscrupulous attempt to save his own skin by hiding behind the shield of the late President, Daugherty explained to a Senate investigating committee that he could not allow himself to be cross-examined because of his friendship with the Harding family. This last was too much for President Coolidge who immediately forced Daugherty to resign his high office. Many critics believe that the President should have ousted Daugherty long before.

Oddly enough, the reaction throughout the country was not that of indignation toward Fall, Doheny, Sinclair and Daugherty—a reaction which would seem to be rational and just. Instead, the newspapers launched a campaign against those gentlemen who had instituted the investigations which had besmirched the reputation of the late President. Senator Walsh was dubbed both "scandal monger" and "character assassin." Such are the perversities of the human mind. And such was the character of the Twenties.

Even the private life of Warren G. Harding was not immune from attack. In 1927, four years after Harding's death, a book entitled *The President's Daughter* was published under the aegis of the "Elizabeth Ann Guild." Written by an unknown, Nan Britton, it sold some 90,000 copies and was the most talked about book of the time. It is estimated that many more thousands of persons read it than bought it, even as reviewers debated whether or not to take note of the manuscript and libraries speculated about the feasibility of purchasing it.

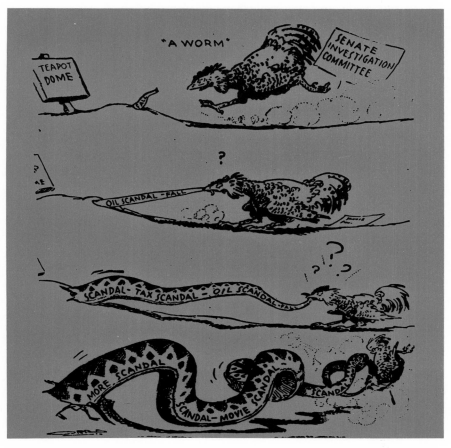

A glimmer of disaster, a shock for Mr. Coolidge, and the demise of "Normalcy."

In this controversial volume, Miss Britton described in breathtaking detail her own romance with Warren G. Harding, a romance which had culminated in the birth of a daughter, Elizabeth Ann Christian, on October 22, 1919 in Asbury Park, New Jersey. The book cited places, names and dates. Miss Britton insisted that her intentions were of the highest order, that she had written the book to ensure "legal and social recognition" of all children born in or out of wedlock. The love letters which Nan Britton assured the world had been written to her by Harding were never disclosed, but it was revealed that the lovely young author had been thoroughly smitten with the great man since 1910, when she was a mere 14 and Harding a supposedly adult 45. According to Miss Britton's account, the affair had begun in 1917 and had continued through Mr. Harding's inauguration. She made much of the fact that she was frequently introduced as Harding's niece and that she had enjoyed a lasting friendship with the late President's wife.

Crime In the Streets, à la 1922. "When will we ever learn?"

The effect upon what remained of Harding's reputation was devastating. Suddenly, the defection into illegality of several Harding friends and appointees seemed more terrible than it had before. In all of the furor that followed, it was fortunate that Mrs. Harding had died several years earlier and was, therefore, spared this last ignobility.

No scandal ever touched the reputation of Calvin Coolidge, the very model of prim, Yankee virtue. Mrs. Alice Roosevelt Longworth is said to have described him as looking as though he had been "weaned on a pickle."

He was not a party boy, believing as he did that, "The business of America is business."

He was a man of conviction rather than passion, and he believed that American prosperity depended upon big business leadership. It was his aim to be the least President possible, and it appears that this aim was accomplished. "Nero fiddled, but Coolidge snored," remarked H. L. Mencken.

The Great Mirage: Keep Cool With Coolidge.

When Coolidge ran for election in his own right in 1924, there was simply no contest between him and his Democratic opponent, John W. Davis. Davis, a native of West Virginia, was selected on the 103rd ballot after a convention deadlock between William Gibbs McAdoo and Alfred E. Smith.

The Democratic party was as badly split in 1924 as it had been in 1920.

In the end, the nation chose to "Keep Cool With Coolidge" —and it voted that way: Coolidge, 15,725,016 votes; Davis, 8,386,503 votes; Progressive Robert La Follette, 4,882,856 votes.

There was little controversy about this inactive administration. One newsworthy occasion arose in 1924 when President Coolidge vetoed the Soldiers' Bonus Bill which involved a cost to the Treasury of the United States of approximately $2 billion. This was anathema to Calvin's parsimonious soul. However, the Senate repassed the Bill over Coolidge's veto, and the President had no choice but to accept it.

Coolidge also had sent the American Marines to Nicaragua to support the incumbent regime against a liberal revolt. As our expansionism within the banana republics increased, the progressive wing of the Republican party objected vociferously. In an unusually shrewd move, Coolidge nominated Dwight Morrow as Ambassador to Mexico, and that capable man managed to undo the damage created by his various predecessors south of the border. In 1928, when Silent Cal murmured demurely that he did not "choose to run" again, the United States enjoyed a better than average relationship with Latin America—a degree of unity which one might envy today.

Throughout Coolidge's five years and seven months in office, the Presidency seemed to function without a President. Times were good and most of America seemed to be content with things as they were. We were ready for an apocalypse.

The Happy Warrior, Alfred E. Smith, surrounded by admirers during his unsuccessful bid for the presidency in 1928.

We lead the WORLD in
1) Wealth
2) Generosity
3) Humility
4) Love of Peace

COPY-BOOK MAXIMS

Q.E.D.

President Coolidge. "AND WHAT IS OUR LOGICAL CONCLUSION FROM THIS, MY FRIENDS? OBVIOUSLY IT IS THAT WE MUST BUILD MORE WAR-SHIPS."

WARREN GAMALIEL HARDING

"Warren, it's a good thing you wasn't born a gal . . . Because you'd be in the family way all the time. You can't say No."
—Dr. George Tryon Harding, speaking to his son.

Warren G. Harding, a man too small for the presidency but big enough to know it, was born to a moderately successful physician's family in 1865 in Blooming Grove, Ohio.

The family, who never made it socially, eventually moved on to Marion, Ohio, where Warren began the long road from smalltime editor and publisher to the White House. Harding succeeded, almost in spite of himself, because he looked the part—he was handsome and distinguished in appearance—and because early in his career he had come to the attention of Harry M. Daugherty, a kingmaker of the first degree who was well known in Republican circles in Ohio and throughout the country. In Harding, Daugherty sensed a winner. From the beginning he played his cards with almost uncanny accuracy.

Harding, who enjoyed a comfortable, if loveless, marriage with the former Florence Kidd, was a lover of women, song and spirits. He indulged these avocations until the end. Despite conventional tastes, a rather limited intelligence, and a spontaneous kindness, he could be and would be manipulated by those whose perspicacity and ambition exceeded his own.

Had it not been for the combined proddings of Daugherty and Mrs. Harding, Warren would probably have ended his days on the Marion *Star,* well-liked in his community, offering and asking for little.

Such was not destiny's plan, nor Daugherty's. Harding left Marion to serve two terms in the Ohio State Senate, then was Lieutenant Governor from 1904 to 1906 and, in 1910, received the Republican nomination for Governor.

In 1914, urged as always by his wife and his mentor, he ran for and was elected to the United States Senate. This was about as far as the Hardings wanted to go. Life in the Senate was not overly demanding. The future president introduced little legislation, enjoyed frequent holidays in Florida, liked the conviviality of the Washington scene. It was a comfortable niche.

In 1916, however, he chaired the Republican National Convention, where the delegates, many of whom were to serve again in 1920, noticed his singular good looks and middle-American charm. Daugherty, always in the wings, took note of this reaction to his protégé.

In 1920, when the Convention reached impasse between its two prime contenders, Frank D. Lowden and General Leonard Wood, Daugherty was on hand to begin the big push. Harding, who had entered the race as Ohio's favorite son only as a means of keeping his (and Daugherty's) grip on the Ohio Republican organization, found himself under serious consideration as a dark horse candidate. It was the last thing in the world that he wanted.

As the balloting went on and on, and as it became clear that Lowden and Wood were hopelessly deadlocked, a meeting of high-ranking Republicans was held in Room 401 of Chicago's Blackstone Hotel—the "smoke-filled room" of political legend. There it was decided that the favorite son from Ohio should have the nomination.

On the tenth ballot, Warren G. Harding, small-town playboy, was duly declared Republican candidate for the presidency of the United States.

It couldn't have happened to a nicer guy, and that was part of the trouble. Kind to animals, kind to children, kind to his cronies, rarely known to utter an acerbic word, Harding won the election by something more like an avalanche than a landslide. He carried 37 states and out-polled his Democratic opponent, James Cox, by 8,000,000 votes. The

country was ripe for a Republican president and Harding's appeal for a "return to normalcy" seemed the perfect antidote to Wilsonian idealism and involvement in foreign affairs.

So Warren G. Harding returned to Washington where he became a figurehead president, bemoaning "My damn friends, they're the ones who keep me walking the floor at night," as he acceded to the whims and desires of those who had manipulated him into office.

In fact, more of his evenings were spent at the poker table than in unhappy floor pacing. Everyone in Washington knew that the upstairs of the White House was a kind of posh saloon. At the "Little Green House" on H Street, which Harry Daugherty shared with his friend Jess Smith, card playing and prohibited liquor were free for all.

The Ohio Gang of hoodlums had a ball, and Harding, fulfilling his father's prophecy, just couldn't bring himself to say No.

On August 2, 1923, President Harding died of a stroke in San Francisco. It was four hours before the news reached the ears of Vice President Coolidge at his home in Vermont. It was several years before the whole story of the fiscal and amorous misadventures of the Harding administration reached the ears of the American people. Harding died a beloved president, whose passing was honestly mourned by the people he "led." When the scandals were fully revealed, even The New York *Times* deplored the besmirching of the man's memory.

Florence Harding had predicted that her husband's election to the presidency would be a "tragedy." It was. And for no one more than for the president himself.

If it is true that a people gets the kind of leadership it deserves, Harding's presidency will always be remembered as Exhibit A. While he sat in the White House with his poker-playing buddies, outside, in hedonistic complacency, the music went on and on.

JOHN CALVIN COOLIDGE

"The business of America
is business."
—Calvin Coolidge

They tell a tale about President Calvin Coolidge, "Silent Cal," a tale about a pretty girl who, seated next to him at dinner, announced that she had a wager with her friends that she could get him to say three words if she tried hard enough. Coolidge turned, fixed his flinty, New England eyes upon the young lady, and said solemnly, "You lose."

Then there's the story about the President's White House interview with football star Red Grange: "Where do you live?" asked Coolidge. "Wheaton, Illinois," replied Grange. "Well, I wish you luck," commented Silent Cal. And that was the end of the meeting.

Colidge did not waste words, at least not in public.[1] In private he was sometimes garrulous or violently temperamental but none but his intimates knew it. Nor did he waste himself. Whatever went on in that unspeaking head of his, we know he equated presidential efficiency with presidential inactivity. At that he was successful.

Nominated for the vice presidency in 1920, neither he nor his wife, the former Grace A. Goodhue—a charming and attractive woman, as outgoing as her husband was reserved —appeared to desire higher office. Their aspirations had extended no further than the Massachusetts Governor's Mansion, which they had occupied before going to Washington. But it was the governorship and his handling of the Boston Police Strike in 1919 which had propelled Coolidge into the public eye and the consciousness of the Republican party. This strike prompted the famous telegram which Coolidge sent to labor leader Samuel Gompers:

"There is no right to strike against the public safety by anybody, anywhere, at any time." For Coolidge, this was a statement of extraordinary eloquence.

[1]Although his small talk was nonexistent, Coolidge did give numerous speeches and held an unprecedented number of press conferences.

The White House years held tragedy for the Coolidge family. Calvin Jr. died from an infection which resulted from a blister on his foot in 1924, an event which almost kept the president from running for office on his own. Mrs. Coolidge, who had enjoyed entertaining in the grand style, curtailed her activities following the death of her son. She occupied herself in an attempt to redecorate the executive mansion with appropriate pieces and saw a limited success in the enterprise which was, much later, carried out effectively by Jacqueline Kennedy.

Grace Coolidge discovered her husband, dead, on the afternoon of January 5, 1933, six months prior to his 60th birthday. America was at the very depth of depression, depression that the New England Yankee had not foreseen.

Small, thin, with reddish hair, the man had never fully recovered from the death of his mother when he was a boy of twelve. Her memory was so much a part of him that when he learned that he had inherited the presidency upon the death of Warren G. Harding, he went, for succor, to his mother's grave.

After the scandals of the Harding years, Coolidge's nomination and election as the 30th President in 1924 were virtually assured. Every element in his Puritanical being contrasted with the flamboyance of his predecessor. Women, for instance.

Other than his mother, Grace was the only female in his life and he treated her coolly. He rarely discussed his problems with her and seemed to disparage her mind—which was a good one. In fact, his treatment of his vivacious lady—the first Presidential consort to smoke—could well be called cruel. Whether this attitude stemmed from his Puritanism or some, murky Freudian Oedipal affliction, no one has yet ascertained. What warmth he had was expended on his sons.

As President, he was patient and he sought to be prudent, but caught up himself in the business optimism of the Twenties he failed to completely recognize that seeds of disaster were being sown and that a great depression was to be the crop.

Calvin Coolidge's silent demeanor was reassuring to a country preoccupied with pleasure, and perhaps a people devoted to rebellion against traditional virtue and restraint of any sort felt comfortable that an arch-conservative such as he could say that government's "greatest duty and opportunity is not to embark on any new ventures."

Born July 4, 1872 and a graduate of Amherst, Coolidge was, for all his failings, a popular president albeit colorless in a colorful age. In a world of gin and sin, Cal preferred to go fishing. In a nation of hilarity, Cal remained taciturn. As economic crisis approached, Cal was unaware. In a consumer's society, Cal was an ecologist of sorts, insisting that glasses replace paper cups, lights be turned off whenever possible, and that reporters provide their own pencils. Such economies were laudable, although his yacht, the Mayflower, cost the citizens of the United States about half a million dollars a year.

The only relief from his model Victorian behavior came about when he got himself up as a cowboy or an Indian for publicity purposes. Even then, he was unsmiling.

ALFRED EMANUEL SMITH

"I recognize no power in the institutions of my church to interfere with the operations of the Constitution of the United States or the enforcement of the law of the land."
—Alfred E. Smith

Al Smith, New York's beloved "Happy Warrior," grew up in poverty on the Lower East Side of Manhattan. The son of a teamster, he left school at 14 to help his family, taking whatever odd jobs he could find. When he turned his hand to politics, Tammany Hall smiled on the energetic man who was to become known for his brown derby hat and his ever-present cigar.

He was a progressive Democrat who earned the ire of the
Republican Party as well as the powerful publisher William
Randolph Hearst. Nevertheless he was elected governor of
New York State in 1918, 1922, 1924, and 1926, and because
he was a reformer of great popularity, received the
Democratic nomination for President in 1928. His name was
put in nomination by Franklin Delano Roosevelt.

Smith had little chance of winning the election. The country
felt secure in its prosperity and was, furthermore, less than
ready for a Roman Catholic president. Adding to the odds
against him, Smith was a dedicated "Wet" in a nation
determined to remain "Dry." As such, he became victim of an
incredible whispering campaign, which dwelled upon the
twin evils of Rum and Romanism. As a people we clung to the
belief that a Catholic president meant the Pope in the White
House, a belief finally laid to rest during the tenure of John
Fitzgerald Kennedy.

Al Smith was deeply hurt by the allegations that he was a
drunkard, a Tammany Tool, a Papal Puppet. It had not
occurred to the innocent governor that his countrymen would
choose to reject him on the basis of his religion. And he was
hurt again when the Democratic Party bypassed him in 1932
to nominate FDR.

A self-made man who achieved financial security, Smith in
later years adamantly opposed U.S. involvement in World
War II, and he did not live to see the final victory. At the time
of his death in 1944 he was actually a Republican
in philosophy.

HENRY LOUIS MENCKEN

"Mencken and Nathan and God;
Yes, probably, possibly, God."
—Elisabeth Cobb

"The man who hates everything" was an epithet flung at
H. L. Mencken.

True, he was an iconoclast. With consummate skill, he aimed
the written word at his enemies: all those who indulged
themselves in hypocrisy, phoniness, sham.

Unlike many intellectuals of the Twenties, Mencken eschewed
the lures of New York City and Paris. Instead, although he
commuted regularly to Manhattan in his role of co-editor (with
George Jean Nathan) of the cogent, irreverent *American
Mercury,* the "Sage of Baltimore," as Mencken was frequently
called, remained entrenched in native Maryland soil. This, he
believed, allowed him to remain in touch with the thoughts of
the rest of America—that great part not bounded by the
Hudson River on the one side and the East River on the other
—the sprawling main section of the country not yet succumbed
to big city thoughts and mores.

New York was, in fact, the object of some of Mencken's more
pointed diatribes. Being away from the city for a good share of
the time allowed him an intellectual immunity from the fads
and fancies of the literary world.

Possessed with a fecund mind and a facile pen, the
well-educated writer and editor was impatient with the foibles
of the self-righteous.

Few were beyond the reach of his verbal puncture. Even the
clergy, also to come under attack in Sinclair Lewis's *Elmer
Gantry,* were open season to Henry Mencken. Sanctimony,
retrogressive sexual ideas, bigotry, fell or at the least were
stunned by his thrust. He fought the prohibitionists, the
fundamentalists—leading off with scathing attacks on William
Jennings Bryan—the Klan. He stood up for all religious
minorities, including atheists, in the name of tolerance.

Where there was smoke, there was Mencken. So threatening was his prose to the Establishment that the Reverend S. Perkes Cadman of Brooklyn appealed to his ministerial colleagues to save college students "from the beliefs preached by H. L. Mencken."

Capable stylist, articulate craftsman, provocative yet careful writer, complete idealist, the man was humble. In *Pistols for Two* he described himself as:

"Five feet eight and one half inches in height and weighs about 185 pounds. In 1915 he bulged up to 197 pounds, then he took the Vance Thompson cure and reduced to 175, rebounding later. He has good eyes and a gentle mouth, but his nose is upset, his ears stick out too much, and he is shapeless and stoop-shouldered. One could not imagine him in the movies. He wears a No. 7 hat. He is bowlegged. He is a fast walker. He used to snore when asleep but had his nasal septum straightened by surgery and does so no longer. He wears BVD's all year round, and actually takes a cold bath every day. He never has his nails manicured, but trims them with a jackknife. He works in his shirt sleeves and sleeps in striped pajamas."

But Mencken was average in appearance only. He was as self-reliant as a Rotarian, energetic as a gadfly, progressive as Robert LaFollette.

Even after he became a topflight editor, he attended trials and political conventions as a reporter. He contributed frequently to the *Baltimore Sun*—one of his numerous successful attempts not to let reality be obscured by glamour.

He was his own man—working toward excellence based upon the standards of taste and judgment he had established for himself. His ability with word and thought were achieved on his own, without the benefit of spoon feeding from someone's professorial chair.

Mencken was anti-neurosis, anti-defeatist, anti-clerical, anti-banal. And, as an inevitable result, he was hated as well and as thoroughly as he was loved.

Those who joined in his crusade against the "Boobus Americanus" (Mencken's term for all who smacked of Babbittism) were countered by those publications which referred to him as "maggot," "hyena," "buzzard" and worse.

Against these abuses, Mencken's virtually flawless logic and meticulous prose stood out in *bas relief*.

He was that singular rarity: an honest human being.

CHAPTER ELEVEN

And All That Jazz

Out of the sordid morass of corrupt politics and politicians, sensationalism and scandal, one facet of the American experience reached an apex during the Twenties it has never again achieved: the world of popular music and the legitimate theatre.

Never before or since have so many actors, playwrights, producers and musicians of real stature emerged during any one decade. It was the "Jazz Age" but very few people knew what jazz was all about.

On stage there were Louis Armstrong, with his magical trumpet, Bix Beiderbecke with his cornet and fabulous band, and Bessie Smith, empress of the blues who, at the time, was virtually unknown to the white population but whose records sold in the hundreds of thousands among blacks. These were jazz figures as great as any the world has known, but they were often reduced to playing in third-rate establishments while the "jazz" orchestra of Paul Whiteman —which combined a bit of syncopation with some schmaltzy violins—gained national prominence and grossed millions. It was a good time to be alive—on either side of the footlights.

George Gershwin, who composed serious music within the "jazz" idiom drew critical scorn for "Rhapsody in Blue" but he was at his melodic best with his scores for "Lady Be Good" and "Of Thee I Sing." Irving Berlin, a most durable composer, wrote such songs as "All Alone," "Blue Skies" and "Remember." Not to be outdone, Vincent Youmans came up with the standards "Tea for Two" and "Hallelujah" among many others.

And as music flowered, so did the theatre. There was something for each taste: the telling dramas of Eugene O'Neill side by side with the sparkling extravaganzas of Florenz Ziegfeld. Relevance and escapism, self-examination and sheer entertainment coexisted peacefully and in abundance.

On stage it was a kind of golden era, one which brought forth glorious stars, glorious music, glorious pageantry. Today, the theatre lover laments the demise of bountiful Broadway. Fifty years ago there was so much to praise, to enjoy, even to idolize, that the stage-struck simply sat back in amazement at the talent and beauty spread before them. There paraded an unending movable feast.

There was Al Jolson, who had an instinctive way of getting to and holding an audience. There were the clowns: the Marx Brothers, Jimmy Durante, Victor Moore, Ed Wynn.

Right—Minorities were beginning to be heard from during the Jazz Age. In 1923 the Pueblo Indians got into the act, gathering on the White House Lawn prior to a hearing before the Senate Lands Committee.

There were the fantastic revues, bringing together talents of every kind—the Music Box, George White Scandals, Garrick Gaieties—all epitomized in the never to be duplicated wonderment of the Ziegfeld Follies.

There were the great performers: Marilyn Miller, Beatrice Lillie, Gertrude Lawrence, Fred and Adele Astaire, and the inimitable Fanny Brice—part comic, part torch singer.

While the world as prewar Americans knew it was going to hell in the handbasket of prohibition and stubborn nationalism, the star-spangled theatre was climbing ever upwards—one of the few real achievements of an age which bore tarnish on practically every enterprise.

It was in the Twenties that Noel Coward reached these shores, bearing his British-born gifts to acting, composing, playwrighting, and simple repartee.

It was a time for a superb revival of the politically pungent works of Gilbert and Sullivan, a time in which child-hating, hard-drinking W. C. Fields burst with all his cynicism into public awareness.

While Daddy and Peaches Browning were making their own peculiar brand of whoopee, while New York Mayor Jimmy Walker was attempting to prove irresponsibility to be an irresistible virtue, while Al Capone was shooting it out with the other thugs in the streets of the Windy City, Jeanne Eagels was playing magnificently in *Rain*. America's most distinguished theatrical dynasty was once again proving its worth as John Barrymore created one of the greatest Hamlets of this or any other century, and the other Barrymores, Lionel and Ethel, proved through their performances in such classics as *Macbeth* and *The Merchant of Venice* that the American stage was a force to be reckoned with. As tribute to the greatness of one of the incredible trio, the Ethel Barrymore Theatre was opened in New York City on December 20, 1928. Few actresses have been so honored.

Eva Le Gallienne, daughter of a poet father and a journalist mother, founded the Civic Repertory Theatre on New York City's 14th Street in 1926, where she produced and acted in more than 30 plays. She was a singular actress, fluent in seven languages and possessed with a profound determination and independence which led her never to marry.

King Oliver's Creole Jazz Band put it altogether—the greatest sidemen of a generation. L to R, Honore Dutry, Baby Dodds, King Oliver, Louis Armstrong, Lillian (Armstrong's future wife), Bill Johnson and Johnny Dodds.

The musical which changed American theatre: "Show Boat," produced
by Florenz Ziegfeld in 1927. Based on a novel by Edna Ferber, with compelling
melodies by Jerome Kern, it is as fresh and beautiful today as it was on
opening night.

The taste of the people embraced everyone from Shakespeare to Georgie Price. Alla Nazimova, born in Yalta, Russia, became an American citizen in 1927, and moved souls in O'Neill's *Mourning Becomes Electra,* which dealt with a plot as old as the ancient Greeks but which under that gifted playwright's talented hand reached new peaks of popularity.

There was such a smorgasbord of talent in all arenas of the legitimate theatre that the mind boggles: Leslie Howard, Florence Reed, Laura Hope Crews who, in *The Silver Cord,* enunciated most of what Philip Wylie had to say about "momism" before that distinguished author had written a published word.

Eugene O'Neill was not the only dramatist of note. Also flourishing were Philip Barry, S.N. Behrman, the marvelously satirical, and sometimes just plain funny Marc Connelly and George S. Kaufman.

There was room for all comers, what with 70 theatres functioning in New York City alone, presenting everything from *Desire Under the Elms* to that indefatigable monument to asininity, *Abie's Irish Rose,* which ran for more than five full years, despite the despair of the critics, most notably Robert Benchley.

The theatre was in its element and the Broadway musical scaled new ramparts with *Show Boat.* This collaboration among Edna Ferber, who wrote the novel on which the play was based, Jerome Kern (music), and Oscar Hammerstein II and P. G. Wodehouse (lyrics) marked a turning point in musical plays. The themes: unhappy marriage and racism— themes not at all popular in the third decade of this century except among the intellectuals. Ours was a culture reared in vaudeville, accustomed to the kickline and to gaud, to the treacly happy endings of Victor Herbert Operettas. There was a place for serious drama, but serious drama with *music?*

Florenz Ziegfeld, that theatrical entrepreneur with his uncanny finger ever on the public pulse—the same Ziegfeld who introduced unprecedented lavishness to the theatre, who had developed the famous Ziegfeld Girls who just stood around the stage looking beautiful—enthusiastically agreed to produce the show. On December 27, 1927, *Show Boat* arrived at the Ziegfeld Theatre to the largest advance ticket sale in history.

It was billed as an "All American Musical Comedy." All American it may have been, including as it did the joys and woes of blacks and whites alike, but "comedy"— perhaps not. To be sure there were funny lines, particularly as delivered by Sammy White and Eva Puck as Frank and Ellie. And there was romance in the characters of

Magnolia and Gaylord, as portrayed by Norma
Terris and Howard Marsh.

But what got to everyone was Helen Morgan's Julie—
the white-looking octoroon whose racial taint spelled
her doom. It was a perfect role for Miss Morgan, whose
own life was filled with tragedy and who, like Julie,
sought any sort of refuge.

Flo Ziegfeld knew what he was about when he selected his American beauties.
The lavishly produced Follies have never been duplicated, never forgotten.
Today Hal Prince is reviving the theme on Broadway—successfully.

Show Boat was the first musical with a message and, as such, was precursor to *South Pacific,* another antiracist musical which filled the houses of the late 40's and early 50's, and *Hair* which, with its own rock beat, repeats the same ideas today, along with some new ones. Musically impressive, thematically inspiring, *Show Boat* has survived numerous revivals and has, somehow, managed to have something important to say almost five decades after its introduction.

The miracle was that, in the thoughtless age of its inception, a musical that said something survived its opening night. Yet when Jules Bledsoe first sang "Ole Man River" before an audience, the future of the Broadway musical was changed forever. Persons who had never before considered the plight of the Southern Negro were moved to compassion and concern—reactions which were long overdue.

It would take many years for this concern to express itself in action, but *Show Boat* had made a start in consciousness-raising at the same time as it was wonderfully entertaining. It was something special in 1927. In 1971, it still is.

Broadway had its well-earned devotees. Still, across the country the motion picture was gaining in popularity, as more and more movie houses opened, competing with each other in opulence of decor.

This variety of entertainment was inexpensive, available to almost everyone, and with it came a whole new way of life and thinking—star-worshiping. The postwar era ached for glamour, and Hollywood—sullied as it was occasionally by the goings-on of such personalities as Roscoe Arbuckle and murdered director William Desmond Taylor, who had consorted with at least two of the country's favorite stars— Mary Miles Minter and Mabel Normand—set about to provide that glamour.

Fearing public reaction to its sins, Hollywood also set about to police itself, setting up Will B. Hayes, Postmaster General during the Harding administration, as arbiter of the public morality. Some of Hayes's notions of what was proper cinematography were to linger for 40 years.

D. W. Griffith, the great director who was responsible for the still honored *Birth of a Nation,* was losing his grip on the public taste, and the laurels fell to one Cecil B. DeMille, originator of the "cast of thousands." He was a master showman who succeeded in producing rather daring films through the ruse of adding moralistic, and often simplistic, endings to his naughty dramas. He relied heavily on the "flashback," combining the new and the old in such a way as to save the sex orgies for the Roman legions, while setting moral examples through his modern, enlightened and usually wealthy heroes and heroines. He found a route which could titillate without offending the sensibilities of his vast audiences.

Fan magazines, with their adoring and frequently less than factual reportage of life among the movie greats, developed an enormous following. Everyone wanted to know about the latest activities of the darlings of the moment. It was important to be aware of the "fact" that Clara Bow, the "IT GIRL," bathed in perfume.

"It" itself became the most important of all commodities.

The creation of one Elinor Glyn, who preferred to be addressed as "Madame Glyn," *It* was the title of one of her short novels. Simply a synonym for sex appeal, Clara Bow was said to have "It" by Miss Glyn herself, and it became fashionable to try to imitate that flatchested, cupid-mouthed young lady on college campuses from Manhattan to Seattle. Clara Bow was, to young women, what Rudolph Valentino, the "Sheik," was to young men.

Hollywood's Big Four, founders of the highly successful United Artists Corporation: L to R—Douglas Fairbanks, Mary Pickford, Charles Chaplin and David Wark Griffith.

The films produced were not limited to sex and sensationalism. Of course there were the "vamps," such as Theda Bara and Nita Naldi—intriguing, mysterious, sexy women who attracted gasps aplenty. But there were also westerns, which seemed to fill a need for adventure in the souls of middle-aged men and young boys alike and which were frequently saddled with such actors as Tom Mix and Bill Hart, both national institutions.

There were serials, dealing with all subjects, engineered to end on a note of crisis so that the viewing public would return to the theatre week after week to see for themselves how these usually inferior little dramas were developing.

There was the enormously talented Charlie Chaplin, whose ability to evoke hilarity and pathos at the same instant has rarely, if ever, been equalled.

There were the "kid stars" like Jackie Coogan. And so many more: Joan Crawford, the flapper's flapper, Lon Chaney, the "Man of a thousand faces," Norma Talmadge, Pola Negri, Gloria Swanson, Dorothy and Lillian Gish, Mary Astor, Corinne Griffith.

The stars were well aware of their status in the public mind and they lived up to their images as well as their considerable incomes would allow. Housed in mansions, chauffeured hither and yon in the most costly of automobiles, bejeweled and begowned, they satisfied the fans' hunger for a dazzling kind of life they could only know vicariously.

Almost overnight, everything in Hollywood changed.

Two of the great stars of the Silent Screen, Charles Chaplin and child star Jackie Coogan in "The Kid," a now-classic movie of 1920.

Al Jolson made a movie in 1927, a movie called "The Jazz Singer," and thus initiated the era of the "talkies." Movies had found a voice.

If some of the major attractions of the decade could bridge the gap—among them Janet Gaynor and Mary Pickford—there were others who could not. Francis X. Bushman, one of the most adored of the great screen lovers, spoke in a high-pitched range which was unsuitable for the new bi-media cinema. His career was at an end. Pola Negri had not a sufficient command of English to make the jump to sound. There were other casualties as well: John Gilbert, Emil Jannings, even Gloria Swanson.

Still, the motion picture was here to stay, although as the thirties came in a new raft of stars appeared on the horizon to take the places of those who would not or could not make the transition to the new way of doing things.

Maybe some theatre piano players were out of work, but no one really wanted to return to dependency on facial expression, body movement and subtitles to tell a tale. Sound was now available, and the public demanded it.

It would take television, and the realization that one could see the stars with his feet up and a beer in his hand to make the motion picture industry sit back and take a serious look at itself.

In the Twenties, however, cinema was the vogue and even spectacular Broadway, with its limited access and high prices, posed no serious threat to its survival.

"The Jazz Singer," himself: Al Jolson in the first "talking" picture. One of the most magnetic personalities in the history of show business, through the medium of recording Jolson will sing again, again and again—hopefully forever.

DAVID WARK GRIFFITH
AND CECIL BLOUNT DEMILLE

". . . The very momentum which he generated carried the industry ahead at a pace which finally left him behind."
—Donald Crisp at
D. W. Griffith's funeral.

David Wark Griffith, the man who made the motion picture into an art form, began his career as playwright and actor. As early as 1907 he had already absorbed a solid decade of stage experience. He had been born into a family of solid background but little cash in 1880 and grew up, stagestruck, in Kentucky.

His early days in the theatre saw him crisscrossing the country —wherever the jobs were. Eventually he decided to earn a living selling story ideas to film studios. He was influenced early by the type of storytelling that characterized *The Great Train Robbery,* and this cinematic approach would show up prominently in his later work.

The Adventures of Dolly, filmed at Biograph's studio on 14th Street, New York City, was a success and thus, with his first plunge into film directing, so was Griffith. He turned out films of high quality in incredible numbers.

Critics believe that his films depicting the contemporary scene surpassed his period dramas but most agree that there was merit in both.

His masterpiece was *The Birth of a Nation* (1915), which cost $100,000 in production and which grossed over $18 million. It was an attempt to tell, impartially, the story of Southern Reconstruction, but it sparked objections. The South didn't much like it, and the Ku Klux Klan was appalled. Griffith, the man who introduced the fade-out, fade-in and flashback, began to realize the true potential of his chosen medium.

With Douglas Fairbanks, Mary Pickford and Charles Chaplin, Griffith established United Artists. As early as 1921, he was toying with the idea of relating sound to motion pictures. In *Dream Street,* a film of that year, he experimented with a sound accompaniment. It was a noble effort but not particularly popular. It would take perfected techniques and the release of *The Jazz Singer* in 1927 to convince the world that sound was here to stay. Charles Chaplin did persist in silent films, releasing *City Lights* in 1931 and *Modern Times* in 1936. For everyone else, silence was no longer golden.

Cecil B. DeMille, who made his first picture, *The Squaw Man,* in 1913 enjoyed a career that lasted well into the Fifties. It was he who popularized the concept of the cast of thousands, and the Massachusetts-born director-producer was a master of the epic sort of production. He had a passion for biblical re-creations, *The Ten Commandments,* which he filmed in 1923 and again in 1956 was one of his all-time triumphs.

If not the artist that D. W. Griffith was, DeMille was a master showman whose movies, from the start, delighted the masses. Some serious movie buffs regard his work with scorn, but it cannot be denied that he glorified the motion picture much as Florenz Ziegfeld glorified the American girl.

As Griffith's career went into decline, DeMille's was still rising. In his final years, the man who made *Birth of a Nation* turned to heavy drinking and deplored what he called the loss of beauty in the film medium.

When he died in 1948 in his rooms at the Knickerbocker Hotel, he was 72. All of Hollywood turned out for his funeral. Charles Chaplin and Cecil B. DeMille were among the honorary pallbearers. DeMille, Griffith's contemporary and sometime rival, outlived him by 11 years.

CHARLES SPENCER CHAPLIN

"The strong men keep coming on,
They go down shot, hanged,
*   sick, broken,*
Call Hallelujah! Call Amen!
*   Call deep thanks!*
The strong men keep coming on."
—Carl Sandberg

Charles Chaplin was one of the most endearing comics ever to grace the motion picture screens of the world but, sadly, for many years his reputation was marred by scandal and vituperation.

Born in London in 1889, Charlie was the son of a show business family who never really made it. His childhood was a miserable one which saw him in slums and orphanages. Tragically, his father, addicted to alcohol, died young and his mother drifted into mental illness. Young Chaplin endured by taking whatever jobs he could find, sometimes on stage, sometimes off.

His biographers believe that he came out of this traumatizing world with an insatiable need for love which was never filled until his 4th marriage, to Oona O'Neill, daughter of the renowned playwright, in the forties.

Although a paternity suit was brought against Chaplin on the eve of the marriage, it is a marriage that has survived—happily, by all reports—and the union has produced eight children. Today the Chaplins live quietly in Switzerland.

Chaplin came to America at the age of 21 and was, in 1920, one of the Hollywood Big Four who established United Artists. Famous for his characterization of the mustached guy in the baggy pants—the unforgettable Little Tramp—he made numerous films, most of which are still intact. The actor himself saved them, down to the discarded footage on the cutting room floor.

Among his notable pictures were *The Gold Rush, City Lights* and *Limelight,* and his talents did not end with acting. He was also a capable writer, director, producer and composer. Chaplin film festivals are in the Seventies nearly as popular as were the Chaplin movies in the Twenties.

In 1924, Chaplin was married for the second time to a sixteen-year-old girl, Lita Gray. It was his second marriage to a teenager and, predictably, it didn't work. However Miss Gray was the mother of Chaplin's oldest sons, Charles Jr. and Sidney—both talented. In his autobiography, Chaplin treats this episode very briefly. Miss Gray's account of the situation is heady reading indeed.

On his third try, Chaplin married actress Paulette Goddard, a Ziegfeld girl *cum* movie star, who was much later wed to novelist Erich Maria Remarque. The Goddard-Chaplin liaison was not publically acknowledged until its dissolution.

Whatever the foibles of Charlie Chaplin's personal and political life, he gave and gives untold joy to millions of persons everywhere. Now, in his later years, he seems at last to have found contentment. He has earned it well.

AL JOLSON

*"Men are marked out from the
moment of birth to rule or
be ruled."*
—Aristotle

No one, it is said in show business circles, ever approached the
magic oneness with an audience that was the special quality
of Al Jolson. No one, that is, except for the late Judy Garland.
From the beginning, the diminutive Jolson never failed to hold
his listeners in the palms of his white-gloved hands.

Those songs that he made famous—among them "Mammy"
and "Sonny Boy"—gripped the people's emotions in a
peculiar and passionate way. This was an era which found the
blackfaced comedian socially acceptable, and it is almost
axiomatic that Al had love and sympathy for black people.
There was no malice in his act. He expressed himself in a form
as right for his time as it would be unfortunate in the 70s.

Born Asa Yoelson in St. Petersburg, Russia, he came with his parents to America while still an infant. From Washington, D.C., where the family settled, Al, as he came to be known, was a perpetual run-away. "Show Biz" was his life. His love of the stage was too much for his fragile resolve to stay at home and play the role of dutiful son.

Papa Yoelson had expected this brown-haired, brown-eyed boy to follow his own career, cantor in a synagogue. But it was a different kind of music which stirred young Asa's soul and would eventually make him undisputed King of American entertainers.

He played in vaudeville, burlesque, revues—gracing the stages of such revered theatrical temples as the Winter Garden and the Palace. Broadway hits including *Honeymoon Express, Sinbad, Big Boy* and *Bombo* became permanently associated with the Jolson name.

While talking pictures trumpeted the demise of some of the great stars—Negri, Valentino, Francis X. Bushman—they provided a whole new metier for Al Jolson. His voice soon became as famous across the land as it had been previously along the Great White Way. All it took was a little movie called *The Jazz Singer*.

Married four times, his third wife was the inimitable Ruby Keeler, who has managed to bridge decades by appearing in 1971 in a spirited revival of *No, No Nanette* which is packing them in as it did in the year of its birth, 1925.

Jolson himself was beloved by several generations. When he died of a heart attack in 1950, he had just returned from entertaining the troops on the front lines of the Korean War. His death was, for many, like the loss of an intimate friend.

That was the magic of the *Jazz Singer,* Al Jolson, the best that Broadway had to offer in a time when talent was abundant.

JAMES J. WALKER

"A good one [politician] is quite as unthinkable as an honest burglar."
—H. L. Mencken, in *Newsweek,* 1955

The Twenties were flamboyant. New York City was flamboyant. Mayor James J. Walker was as flamboyant a personality as the world has yet produced.

Elected in 1925, by a margin of 400,000 votes over his Republican opponent, Frank D. Waterman, Jimmy Walker rarely let his administrative responsibilities interfere with his real goal in life: the pursuit of pleasure. It seemed as though the mayoralty was a springboard from which to achieve fun, and still more fun, until the fun in "Fun City" eventually ran out.

A flashy, free-wheeling, high-living man, Walker became a kind of folk hero—a hero whose life was to be an on-going musical comedy, devoid of substance but brimming over with chutzpah. The beautiful people of his day adored him.

The problems of high office appear to have worried him not at all. Often on vacation, late to nearly every official appointment, openly involved with his mistress, actress Betty Compton, rarely at his desk in City Hall before noon, writing songs instead of keeping the lid on New York, Walker could only have survived politically in a time as hedonistic as that in which he lived and flourished.

A 20th century Nero, who fiddled away his energies as New York City burned, a dandy who changed his clothing three times daily, "Beau James" expended his talents on the ladies and the nightclubs, while Tammany Hall, unchecked, soaked the City as thoroughly as it could be soaked, which was considerably.

To Walker, life was a merry-go-round, and he had the golden ring clasped securely in his manicured hand.

In 1929, Fiorello La Guardia, about as rumpled as Jimmy Walker was debonaire, put up a worthy fight for City Hall, but the times were not right for the man who would one day become the greatest mayor New York City has ever known. La Guardia lost each of the city's 62 election districts, to the happy-go-lucky incumbent, Mr. Walker.

Everything changes. Soon after Walker's re-election came the Crash and, with it, the demise of his staggering popularity.

Hungry people were not receptive to his shallow obsession with all that glistered, little of which was gold. Indulgent smiles of understanding soon turned to grimaces of confused concern.

With the exposé of his corrupt government, New Yorkers came to know that Walker's boyish tomfoolery was out of place in a suddenly sobered and subdued world.

A man was needed for the job, and New Yorkers knew where to find him. In 1933, Fiorello La Guardia, the memorable "Little Flower," was elected mayor. The hoopla was over, and a great metropolis began to reassess its values.

FANNY BRICE

*"—and with honesty goes
another thing: that you don't
like things in [other] people
that you don't like in yourself."*
—Fanny Brice

There were three great loves in Fanny Brice's life: the theatre, her second husband—a gambler named Nick Arenstein—and her children. She was an outrageous comic with uncompromising standards and values, honesty and hard work among them. To no one did she apply her standards as unrelentlessly as she did to herself.

She was Florenz Ziegfeld's greatest star, knew it, and was never overly impressed by the knowledge. Perhaps it is her combination of self-confidence and humility which makes her a legend even in the 1970s.

Those who are over 30 remember her hilarious deadpan radio characterizations of "Baby Snooks," a naughty little girl invented by Fanny herself. Those who are over 60 remember, if they are fortunate, her broad Broadway comedy routines. They remember, also, the haunting song "My Man," which came out of the Ziegfeld Follies of 1921-22, and which Fanny embraced as her own—testifying as it did to her unswerving loyalty to Nick Arenstein, whom she finally divorced in 1927 after she had stood by him while he did time in Leavenworth.

Those who don't remember came to know and love Fanny through Barbara Streisand's outstanding recreation of her personality in the stage and screen versions of *Funny Girl,* a play which recorded her early days with unusual accuracy.

Pretty, Fanny was not. Talented, she was. On the surface, the saloon keeper's daughter, born Fannie Borach, lived a life of jazz, pizazz, and plenty of good luck. As with so many illusions, this one, too, was a fraud. She was a star—a fabulous star—who parlayed her very lack of good looks into top billing. Doing her famous "Dying Swan" parody of the ballet, looks didn't matter. As "Baby Snooks," her rare facial grimaces were half of the act. When she got down to singing that song which she immortalized, she was the embodiment of every disappointed woman since Eve. Prettiness was unimportant. She was beautiful.

The comedienne, born in 1891, grew up on the Lower East Side of Manhattan, in Newark, N.J. and in Brooklyn. Although the reports of her early poverty are largely exaggerated, the road to Ziegfeld was neither slow nor easy. She was a childhood scamp who sometimes begged on the streets—so enchanted was she with the act of woebegone hunger she employed in order to relieve some well-dressed gentleman from a modicum of his bankroll.

She came up the hard way, through amateur nights (which she frequently won), burlesque and vaudeville. Once Ziegfeld caught her act in 1910 she was on her theatrical way, and she never stopped outdoing even herself until she died.

The only disaster of her career in entertainment was *Fanny,* her one attempt at a straight play.

Unlucky in love—all three of her marriages ended in divorce, including an amicable parting from showman Billy Rose who, tired of being dubbed "Mr. Brice" was impelled to make himself a legend too (and he doubtless would have succeeded without that prodding)—she was at her best on stage and in her own home.

She was flippant, gay, a good cook, a horse player, who cherished her friends and disliked nightclubs. Money was never of much interest to her. She didn't bother to count it. But when she died in 1951, she left behind about $2 million, along with memories of warmth, bravery, earthiness and homespun wisdom.

Fanny Brice was one of those rare celebrities who despite the downs of her private life—and there were several of them— was a success both as a star and as a human being.

FLORENZ ZIEGFELD

".... A combination of P. T. Barnum, John W. Gates, David Belasco and Get-Rich-Quick Wallingford."
—The New York Graphic

Florenz Ziegfeld was the greatest producer of all time. He was known as the "Great Glorifier" of the American girl, for he discovered the most beautiful young women in the land and then proceeded to play on their best features. He was known as a star-maker, and stars he made: Anna Held, Marilyn Miller, Billie Burke, Fanny Brice, Eddie Cantor, Will Rogers and W. C. Fields among them.

Thrift was a quality unknown to Flo, but his extravaganzas were always in good taste. He seemed to realize, whether selecting showgirls or comics, just what the American public wanted at any particular moment. He always provided it.

Born in Chicago in 1869, Ziegfeld was a master at public relations. Always willing to take chances, he insisted upon opulence. To him, packaging was of prime importance, and the effect of that thinking influenced his personal life. If he passed an outstanding picture window, he would frequently purchase whatever was there displayed, whether he needed it or not.

He was contradictory, as are most people—great or not so great. He had six cars, several private telephone lines, but he loved also the solitude of fishing and enjoyed rapport with his Indian guides.

He was married twice, first to Anna Held, the actress, who divorced him in 1913 but loved him until the end of his days. He was wed again, in 1914, to Billie Burke, another Ziegfeld star. His one child, Patricia, was a product of that marriage. She attests that for all the turbulence of the union, hers indeed was a happy childhood. The marriage was terminated only by Ziegfeld's death in 1932.

Along with the "Follies" and the "Midnight Follies" which were presented on the roof of the New Amsterdam Hotel, Ziegfeld produced *Sally* in 1922 for the lovely, but doomed, Marilyn Miller. Later came *Sunny* and *Rosalie,* in which Miller also starred, and *Rio Rita.* He was always willing to try something new, to spend the extra energy and extra cash to lift his productions as high as they could go.

Softspoken and gentle, a small man in physical stature only, Florenz Ziegfeld crowned his spectacular career with his production of *Show Boat* in 1926. This was a radical departure from what had gone before in the musical theatre but, as everyone knows, it is still popular, still in demand, still relevant. (Chapter 12.)

He was capable of spending $3 million on three shows—an incredible figure for the Twenties—and of losing $100 thousand in a single evening at the baccarat tables. But financial misfortune overcame him at last. The Great Ziegfeld never recovered from the stock market crash in 1929. The last "Follies" he produced was made possible only through the combined contributions of his loyal employees and his wife, Billie Burke, who had accumulated a fair sum in her own right.

After his death, former collaborators Jerome Kern, Otto Harbach, Irving Berlin, Oscar Hammerstein, and Sigmund Romberg, purchased rights to 72 Ziegfeld shows for only $28,000 at auction.

He died insolvent, but still knowing where his heart was. In the last few days of his life, lying helpless in a hospital bed, he created a show in fantasy—ordering proper music, proper lighting, proper placement in "the line" of the glorious Ziegfeld girls. It was heartbreaking, but it was the last gasp of Ziegfeld's soul.

He was a creation of his own time, who took what happened to be at hand, coupled it with enormous vision and energy, and left behind him stars so grateful and devoted that Will Rogers, for one, was shattered to the point of tears at his passing.

As epitaph, it is enough to remember him and to remember that his name was Zieg*feld.* It was Flo's particular concern that everyone knew him, yet so few could pronounce the name that glamorized a generation.

MARY PICKFORD AND DOUGLAS FAIRBANKS

"America's Sweethearts"

Mary Pickford, perennial little girl, was the darling of the Jazz Age. She represented the appealingly innocent little thing next door, rather than the chic and rather brazen flapper. She was lovely to look at. And she could act, in a genuine sort of way that set her apart from the rest of the Hollywood crowd, at a time in which it was fashionable to emote.

In 1920 she was married to the handsome, swashbuckling Douglas Fairbanks, and the moviegoing public went virtually out of its mind with joy. The event had received plenty of advance publicity in the avidly devoured fan magazines, and the wedding itself was the romantic event of the year.

Together, this talented pair came close to making Hollywood socially acceptable. Off screen and on they were the heroine and hero of adoring worshippers, those who had come to need someone to look up to at about that time.

While Mary was, onstage, the epitome of the adorable ingenue, Douglas began in comedy and then went on to enchant the public with an amazing array of athletic accomplishments which were used to their fullest in the motion pictures in which he starred.

He always got the girl.

Together, these two stars created "Pickfair," an antique-filled mansion surrounded by 15 acres in Beverly Hills, with a commanding view of that suburb and the city of Los Angeles which stretched beyond.

An around-the-world tour, which the two embarked upon in 1926, netted them a museum-like collection of *objets d'art,* including rare Oriental dishes and weaponry, and the china which, allegedly, an earlier hero, Napoleon, presented to his Empress, Josephine.

Douglas Fairbanks died some years ago, and with him died the epoch which allowed Mary Pickford to collect her friends and all manner of gourmet goodies and set off on horseback toward the Pacific, passing hardly a house along the way.

The opulence at Pickfair still exists for the star of *Little Lord Fauntleroy* and *Pollyanna.* At 78, married to the protective and adoring Buddy Rogers as she has been for more than 30 years, Mary remains largely confined to her bedroom, reclusive in an atmosphere she created for herself many long years ago. She lives out her days in a room with multiple windows which look out over the city where she reigned as undisputed queen.

She was the greatest and most beloved movie star of the Twenties, and she had the intelligence to retire in time—an intelligence shared by too few show business personalities. She was also a shrewd businesswoman who, along with Mr. Fairbanks and Charles Chaplin, was a co-founder of United Artists, a ploy through which these entertainers were to boost their profits enormously.

What she thinks of the "good old days" in the cinema is her own secret. She doesn't watch old movies (especially not her own), does not care for television, reads Shakespeare for fun.

It is often a tragedy to outlive one's friends and colleagues but through her long-lived (by show business standards) marriage to Mr. Rogers, the sweetheart of America seems to have found a comforting port in which to enjoy old age.

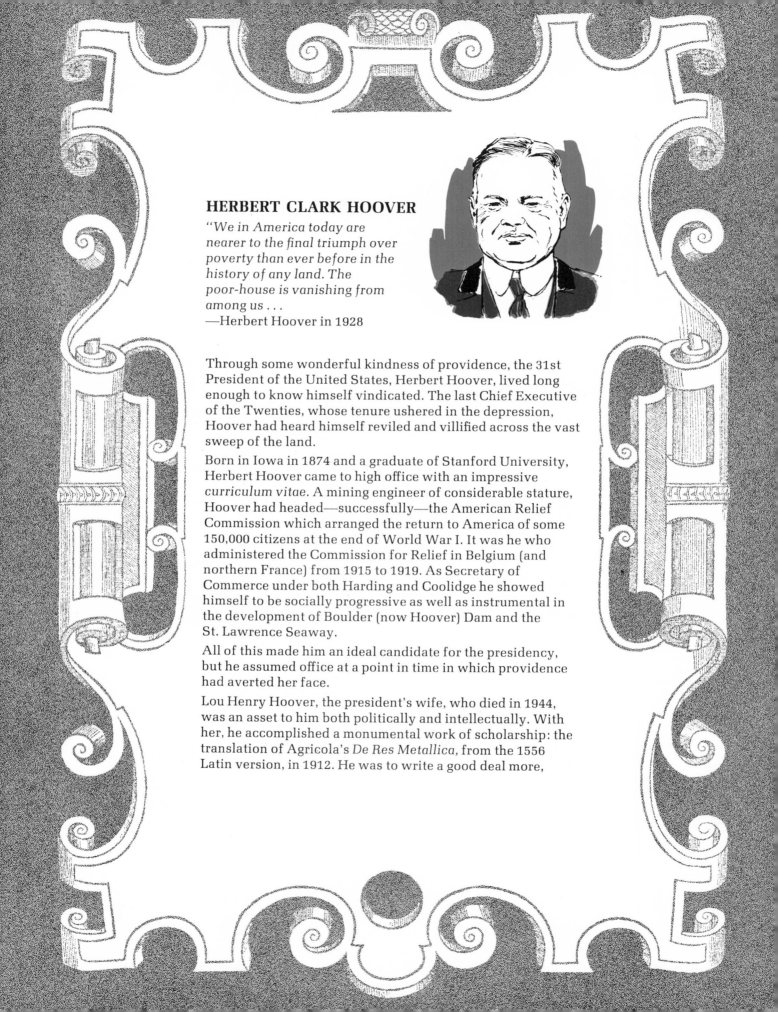

HERBERT CLARK HOOVER

"We in America today are nearer to the final triumph over poverty than ever before in the history of any land. The poor-house is vanishing from among us . . .
—Herbert Hoover in 1928

Through some wonderful kindness of providence, the 31st President of the United States, Herbert Hoover, lived long enough to know himself vindicated. The last Chief Executive of the Twenties, whose tenure ushered in the depression, Hoover had heard himself reviled and villified across the vast sweep of the land.

Born in Iowa in 1874 and a graduate of Stanford University, Herbert Hoover came to high office with an impressive *curriculum vitae*. A mining engineer of considerable stature, Hoover had headed—successfully—the American Relief Commission which arranged the return to America of some 150,000 citizens at the end of World War I. It was he who administered the Commission for Relief in Belgium (and northern France) from 1915 to 1919. As Secretary of Commerce under both Harding and Coolidge he showed himself to be socially progressive as well as instrumental in the development of Boulder (now Hoover) Dam and the St. Lawrence Seaway.

All of this made him an ideal candidate for the presidency, but he assumed office at a point in time in which providence had averted her face.

Lou Henry Hoover, the president's wife, who died in 1944, was an asset to him both politically and intellectually. With her, he accomplished a monumental work of scholarship: the translation of Agricola's *De Res Metallica*, from the 1556 Latin version, in 1912. He was to write a good deal more,

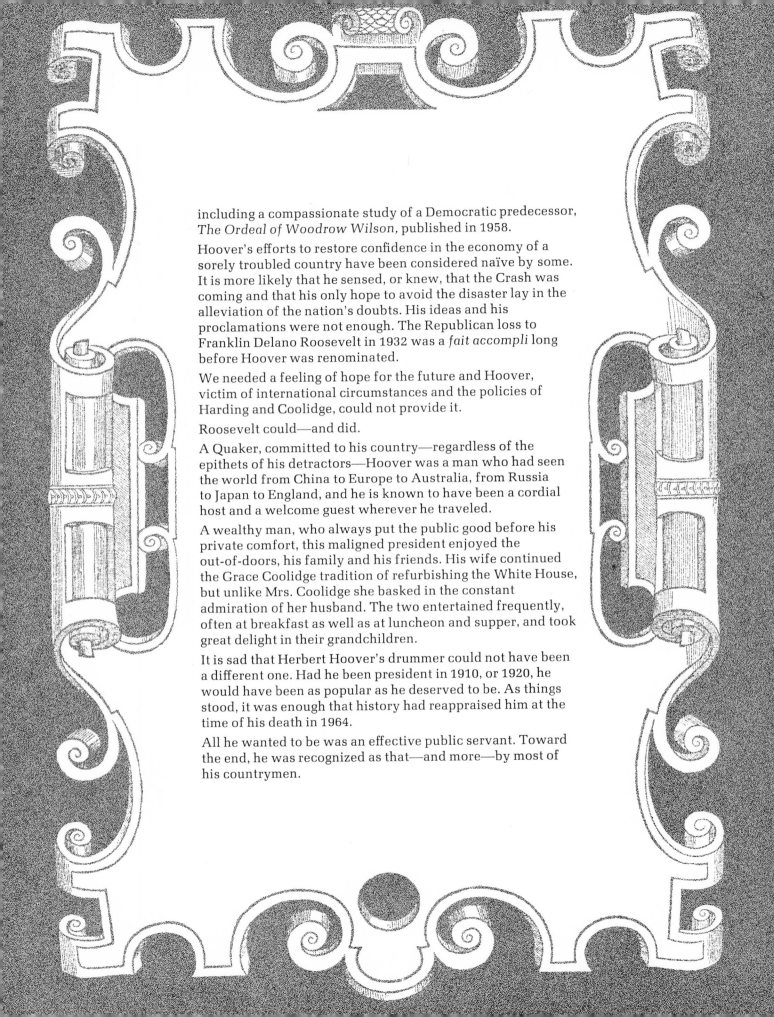

including a compassionate study of a Democratic predecessor, *The Ordeal of Woodrow Wilson,* published in 1958.

Hoover's efforts to restore confidence in the economy of a sorely troubled country have been considered naïve by some. It is more likely that he sensed, or knew, that the Crash was coming and that his only hope to avoid the disaster lay in the alleviation of the nation's doubts. His ideas and his proclamations were not enough. The Republican loss to Franklin Delano Roosevelt in 1932 was a *fait accompli* long before Hoover was renominated.

We needed a feeling of hope for the future and Hoover, victim of international circumstances and the policies of Harding and Coolidge, could not provide it.

Roosevelt could—and did.

A Quaker, committed to his country—regardless of the epithets of his detractors—Hoover was a man who had seen the world from China to Europe to Australia, from Russia to Japan to England, and he is known to have been a cordial host and a welcome guest wherever he traveled.

A wealthy man, who always put the public good before his private comfort, this maligned president enjoyed the out-of-doors, his family and his friends. His wife continued the Grace Coolidge tradition of refurbishing the White House, but unlike Mrs. Coolidge she basked in the constant admiration of her husband. The two entertained frequently, often at breakfast as well as at luncheon and supper, and took great delight in their grandchildren.

It is sad that Herbert Hoover's drummer could not have been a different one. Had he been president in 1910, or 1920, he would have been as popular as he deserved to be. As things stood, it was enough that history had reappraised him at the time of his death in 1964.

All he wanted to be was an effective public servant. Toward the end, he was recognized as that—and more—by most of his countrymen.

EUGENE O'NEILL

*"The people who succeed
and do not push on to a greater
failure are the spiritual
middle classers."*
—Eugene O'Neill

The American theatre reached its pinnacle in the works of
playwright Eugene O'Neill, considered by many to be the
greatest dramatist this country has yet produced. His
particular glory was to raise the show business I.Q. of the
theatre-going public above the stunning mediocrity of
vaudeville [fine as it was in its own way) to the level of serious
writing that could hold its own with Shakespeare and Shaw.

It is not necessary to be serious at all times and in all pursuits,
but it was O'Neill who made it clear that the stage was big
enough to accommodate real persons with real problems as
well as jugglers, showgirls and rhythmic music.

Nervous, frequently profoundly unhappy, O'Neill dared in his
prolific output of plays to sweep away some of the more
cherished cobwebs of the collective conscience. For this he has
earned the thanks of every major actor and playwright
to follow him.

In the Twenties alone, he was to write more than 20 plays,
most of which dealt with themes considered daring at the time,

and three of which were to be awarded Pulitzer prizes.

The dramatist drew upon his careful observations of his fellow man as well as upon his own background. Born in 1888, the son of a romantic actor James O'Neill, he attended a variety of boarding schools and, for one year, Princeton University. This was but the beginning of his education. After Princeton, he traveled, searched for gold, did an inevitable stint as a reporter, all the time collecting and retaining material for what would be his life's work.

He developed a feeling of empathy with the misfits of this world, obviously numbering himself among them.

In 1912, after a bout with tuberculosis, Eugene O'Neill settled down to serious playwrighting. *Beyond the Horizon* in 1920 firmly established his reputation in the theatre. With astonishing speed, there followed *Diff'rent* (1920), *The Emperor Jones* (1920), *Anna Christie* (1921) and, among many others, *Desire Under The Elms* (1924), which explored the battle for dominance between a father and his son, and *Strange Interlude* (1928), a study of homosexuality which ran for five full hours.

A winner of a Nobel Prize in 1936, O'Neill will also be remembered as the father of Oona O'Neill Chaplin, wife of quite a different sort of genius, but a genius nevertheless.

O'Neill died in 1953 in New York City.

CHAPTER TWELVE

Prosperity Persists

Florida was the place to go during the Coolidge years—no longer just a winter haven for the big rich, but a retreat for the average family.

Swamps suddenly were transformed into pseudo-Venetian lagoons, William Jennings Bryan lounged under a beach umbrella and eulogized the beauty of the Florida landscape and climate, real estate became the big business of this Southern state. It was such a big business that in the summer of 1925, at the very peak of the Florida Boom, a single issue of the Miami *Daily News* was swollen to more than 500 pages, simply to accommodate all of the real estate advertisements.

The "boom" at crest, as the beaches of Miami attracted hordes of winter weary Northerners.

Now that the auto had made us a mobile people, now that the majority experienced a new prosperity, it was possible to escape some of the rigors of the Northern winter. Thus, Florida.

Its roads were jammed with cars in the early part of 1925, and those who did not drive to Elysium came by sea, by train, or even, occasionally, on foot. Miami had grown in the short span of 25 years from a population of 10,000 to 150,000 and it confidently anticipated a population of one million by the mid-thirties.

Choking the arteries of a nation, the rapid growth of automobile traffic contributed to a revolution in manners and morals.

Orange groves were destroyed so that home sites could be provided.

Settlements sprang up along the 300-mile stretch of highway which connected Jacksonville with Miami in such close concentration that the effect was that of a 1920's style linear city.

Subdivisions grew up everywhere; the hard sell was a frequently utilized instrument of persuasion; free lunches and free rides were provided to lure the crowds to the mushrooming developments.

Overall, in only five years the population of the State had increased by fifty per cent, and the winter-tired eyes of the world turned to Flagler Street, Miami, a thoroughfare so jammed with cars from out-of-state as to be virtually impassable.

The Hialeah Express. In a latter day version of the wagon train, "live ones" were driven through Florida to be lured into real estate purchases.

Dissent existed in this best of all possible worlds. Police, not then considered Pigs, confronted striking textile workers of Paterson, N.J. in 1926.

People would buy anything, so long as it were in Florida—
and they would buy whether they had seen the property or
not. The idea was to escape the industrial intensity of
prosperity, to linger in the tropical sun, to get away from it
all. So many nibbled at the bait that Florida became the
embodiment of that which its immigrants were attempting
to escape.

Taking its cue from Southern California, drawing upon its
convenience to the big cities of the North, Florida was rising
high—until it reaped the whirlwind.

Investors frequently defaulted on their payments.
Others suddenly discovered that Florida was not immune
from rain and cold. The denouement was brought about
by two crushing hurricanes.

It was Chicago, 1929, when seven members of George (Bugs) Moran's gang
received their final valentines. Al Capone's favored trigger man, Jack McGurn,
was indicted for this gift from Cupid, but the St. Valentine's Day Massacre
was never brought to trial.

Early in the morning of September 18, 1926, the second, and by far the more severe, of these hit the Miami area, bringing about untold destruction, ruining the newly created suburbs, leaving 400 persons dead and more than 50,000 homeless.

The promoters and speculators tried desperately to save their child, but Florida no longer looked like Shangri-la, and Shangri-la was what the people wanted. Boom had turned to bust. Most averted their eyes from reality, but Florida was a symptom of what was to come.

In the beginning gasoline pumps were a bit of a novelty, but within a few years they were destined to dot the American landscape like a permanent measle epidemic.

Although Calvin Coolidge seemed not to have recognized the economic clouds gathering upon the national horizon, Mr. Hoover, somewhat more astute, was aware that our position as a prosperous country was precarious. Even his numerous detractors have rarely questioned Hoover's intelligence. Yet, it was he who was to preside over disaster.

Common stocks had soared in price since 1924, and cautious brokers and bankers were advising their clients that a peak had been reached, that Utopia could not last forever, that eventually something would have to give.

As much as a year earlier, the Federal Reserve System had lowered the rediscount rate from 4 to $3^1/2$ percent, hoping that by easing money rates America would cease to accumulate the huge quantities of gold which were depleting European coffers—a move designed to increase international trade and to assist in European recovery.

Inflation was rampant. While stock prices rose, business was falling off. Such conservative observers as the Harvard Economic Society, Moody's Investor Service and *The New York Times* were urging caution.

But few heeded these serious voices. The little man wanted a piece of the action of the big bull market, and he was going after it—the voices of discretion be damned.

On March 3, 1928, the stock market began its fantastic zoom to the top, a top which would in the long run prove to be the bottom—for practically everybody.

Shortly before the election of 1928, the United States, along with 14 other nations, signed the Pact of Paris (The Kellogg-Briand Pact) which was conceived to eliminate war. As a national policy, armed conflict was to be a thing of the past except in cases of self-defense. It was an expression of America's hope for world peace and a confirmation of America's optimism.

And so, with the election of the dedicated and able Herbert Hoover, a man who compensated in administrative aptitude for what he lacked in charisma, over the Happy Warrior, Alfred E. Smith, we were still experiencing what had come to be known as "Coolidge Prosperity." The sagging markets of 1920 and 1921 were long since overcome. Marcus Garvey, the self-styled Provisional President of Africa, had been convicted five years before for illegal use of the mails. Most intellectuals had fled to Paris. There were few remaining voices of dissent. "Peace and Prosperity" were the ideals desired by everyone, and the ideals which most people thought had been achieved.

Hoover's election was assured for three reasons: It was a Republican decade (after all, things were just fine, weren't they?); Al Smith was a Roman Catholic (and that meant the danger of the Pope running the White House, didn't it?); and, it is believed, the women of America, exercising their eight-year-old prerogative, wanted and voted for a "dry" president.

But there were sharks under the surface of the seemingly serene sea. There were signs everywhere that the world was no longer the oyster of the United States. The farmer had never shared in the prosperity enjoyed by the businessman. Prices were rising rapidly. Speculators were brazenly operating in Wall Street.

A Chicken *for* Every Pot

o York Tim

ORK, TUESDAY, OCTOBER 29, 1929.

mory Honored
Fete on Ships

and in port offi-
Navy Day yester-
major land cele-
ld on Sunday, the
he birth of Theo-
imilar ceremonies
re reserved for

as kept by ships
ublic was invited
Flags appropriate
broken out on all
s, and even some
t in the harbor
nts in honor of

les and the new
ble and other
craft at Lake-
rdered out and
ng the Atlantic
er this city and

E. BURTON,
DIES AT 77

EUROPE IS DISTURBED
BY AMERICAN ACTION
ON OCCUPATION DEBT

London Urges an Explanation
of Move for Direct Payments
by Germany.

BANK'S PRESTIGE INVOLVED

Britain and Continent Feel That
We Do Not Have Faith in
Young Plan Institution.

SCHEME IS LAID TO HOOVER

President Is Said to Wish to Avoid
Clash in Congress Over Linking of
Reparations and War Debts.

STOCK P
IN NATI
BANK

Sixteen Leading
Tel. & Te

A shrinkage of
shares of sixteen repr
sweeping decline on t
American Teleph
$448,905,162 having be
Steel common, traditi
greatest nose-dive in
a low of 185. In a f
at which it closed, sh
sented for the 8,131,0
loss in value of $142,2
In the following
the outstanding share

Issues.
American Radiator

Photo Credits

the slings and arrows of outrageous Rogers rarely missed their marks.

He nearly always refused to take political sides, looking upon the news only as a source of new material for his act. Yet, being an Oklahoman he was, in name at least, a Democrat.

From vaudeville, Rogers went on to movie acting and column writing. His audience, no longer confined to the limitations of a small theatre, grew as his career expanded. Somehow, the voice that had sardonically expressed the concerns of the Southwest struck up a response in the good people of the far and middle west as well. He even got through to jaded Easterners.

Writer, traveler, actor, showman, Will Rogers was a man for all American seasons. An entertainer who resolutely avoided blue comedy, he found himself an endearing and enduring part of the United States scene.

When, in 1935, Rogers undertook a flight with his friend, pilot Wiley Post, a flight intended to terminate in the Orient, the entire country mourned the loss of the comedian's plane. In an age in which nastiness was considered a special kind of virtue, Rogers' kindly wisdom would long be missed. If he had never known a man he did not like, perhaps it was because there were few, if any, who did not like him.

He was what was needed in Fitzgerald's Jazz Age: a homespun, gum-chewing, lariat-twisting, gentle man of great strength, who offset gaud and glitter with a kindliness and subtle humor (often masking profound truths) which provided contrast from the spangled nonsense that suffused most of the country.

Born in what was to become Oklahoma in 1879, Will Rogers grew up on one of the last frontiers. He was part Cherokee Indian, a fact which delighted him so that he often called upon it in his comedy routines.

Rogers, who received the bulk of his education from McGuffey's well-distributed readers, is said to have created the image of a far greater illiteracy than he actually possessed. Despite the mythmakers, it is known that he did attend school, including Kemper, a Missouri-based military academy, and that it was not until 1898 that this lonesome cowboy left school once and for all.

A low-keyed comedian, about as universally loved as it is possible to be in this land of diversity, Will came to show business as a wild west rider in 1902.

By 1915, he had joined the Ziegfeld Follies—about as far as one could go in those days—where he parlayed the *faux pas* of his constituency into fame and, ultimately, fortune. The august bodies of government were frequently his targets, and

WILL ROGERS

*"All I know is what I read in
the papers."*
—Will Rogers

In the Seventies, a man who never met anyone he did not
like would be open to suspicion, if not to genuine hostility.
But Will Rogers said it, and with sincerity—a characteristic
which would lead many modern men to scorn. Sincerity
today is often reflected in a muted club tie, and is perhaps
found, if ever, in some of the more enlightened hippie
communes, or in certain rare interpersonal relationships.

Maybe because of his times or, perhaps, due to his inherently
kind personality, Will Rogers mouthed his platitudes and they
did not seem platitudinous at all. He got away with it and, in
the bargain, gained the affection of a nation.

In 1918, already an elderly man, Debs was sentenced to 10 years in prison for violation of The Espionage Act—a law designed to repress antiwar activities prior to and during America's involvement in World War I.

Debs was by no means a newcomer to controversy. A former railroad man, he was founder of the American Railway Union and, in 1894, had managed to prevent magnate James J. Hill from reducing the pay of employees on the Great Northern. Convicted of violating an injunction in 1895, despite the efforts of Clarence Darrow, Debs spent six months in jail. In his middle 60s, he entered the State Penitentiary at Moundsville, Virginia in April, 1919. Later he was removed to the Federal Prison in Atlanta, Georgia. It was from a prison cell that Debs, No. 9653, made his last effort for the presidency.

In 1921, Woodrow Wilson, stripped through illness of many of the rational qualities he had once possessed, was adamant in his refusal to grant a pardon to Debs, regardless of the proddings of Attorney General A. Mitchell Palmer, of all people. Wilson's attitude was a strange one for a man committed to a just and lasting peace. Debs's crime had been to cling to the doctrine of noninterventionism, a classic American policy.

Ironically, it was President Warren G. Harding who eventually effected Debs' release. His health broken, the gentle-spoken Socialist returned to his native Indiana for Christmas, 1921, and there he lived quietly with his wife, Kate, until his death in October, 1926.

EUGENE VICTOR DEBS

*"I would a thousand times
rather be a free soul in jail than
to be a sycophant and coward
in the streets."*
—Eugene V. Debs

The flat, prairie town of Terre Haute, Indiana, does not appear to be a likely spawning ground for a revolutionary or even a socialist. Yet, in 1855, it produced one in the person of Eugene V. Debs, who was destined to run for the presidency in 1900, 1904, 1908, 1912 (when as Socialist candidate he polled nearly a million votes) and in 1920. The record shows that he was never really in the race, but he inspired an almost mystical devotion on the part of his followers.

The Rockefellers tried to save the market through astute purchasing and reassuring admonitions to the public. It was too late for, as comedian Eddie Cantor said, who but the Rockefellers had any money left?

Since 1924, America had enjoyed a bull market. There had been a mild depression in 1920-21, but it principally affected only the farmers. For several years fortunes were made, spent, reinvested, blown. Everyone wanted a slice of the pie, nearly everyone adopted the "get rich quick" philosophy which gripped the nation. Formerly the milieu of the rich and the comfortably well-off, the Stock Market now attracted the little man, who gambled all he had and more— on margin. Margin meant, simply, that when one borrowed money to buy, what was bought was offered as collateral for the loan. It was the undoing for many.

In September, 1929, the Market was at its highest crest. As stocks soared, predictions that it couldn't last were ignored. And then, suddenly, it was sell, sell, sell while the calls went out at a frantic pace.

Herbert Hoover offered his reassurances, as did Andrew Mellon. We needed more than reassurance.

Things came to a climax on Black Tuesday, 1929, when the bottom dropped out of Wall Street—a street which now held the futures of the middle class as well as of the wealthy.

Only some feeble jokes remained.

Will Rogers said, "You stand in line to get a window to jump out of." And suicides there were, because not only had the nation's paper profits disappeared, investors great and small wiped out, but the prosperous Twenties were at an end. The age of prosperity had given way to a tangible austerity. An era had ended, with a bang, not a whimper. All that remained of the Jazz Age was a people looking nostalgically backward as they took their places in the breadlines. Disaster was reality.

The debacle of the Crash sent thousands onto the streets to wander about in gloom and disbelief.

Every drama has its final curtain. That of the Twenties came down spectacularly, to a dimmed house—unsuspecting, unaware, content with buying stock "on margin" in what most thought of as a time of unparalleled prosperity. That it was, for some. Not for the migrant worker, not for the black, not for the civil servant, but for some.

1929 was the year of disaster, the year in which some 40 percent of the total valuation of stocks was lost. This meant billions of dollars.

Marches are not indigenous to the 1970's. Even in the 20's the people would be heard.

**es.**

TWO CENTS In Greater New York | THREE CENTS Within 200 Miles | FOUR CENTS Elsewhere Except 7th and 8th Postal Zone

CES SLUMP $14,000,000,000
N-WIDE STAMPEDE TO UNLOAD;
RS TO SUPPORT MARKET TODA'

ues Down $2,893,520,108;
nd Steel Among Heaviest Losers

03,520,108 in the open market value of the ntative companies resulted from yesterday's New York Stock Exchange.

and Telegraph was the heaviest loser, opped off of its total value. United States bellwether of the stock market, made its nt years by falling from a high of 202½ to . last-minute rally it snapped back to 186, g a net loss of 17½ points. This represhares of common stock outstanding a total 46.

e are shown the day's net depreciation in the sixteen companies referred to:

	Losses in		
Shares Listed.	Points.	Depreciation.
...... 10,096,289	10⅜	$104,748,997

PREMIER ISSUES HARD H

Unexpected Torrent
Liquidation Again
Rocks Markets.

DAY'S SALES 9,212,80

Nearly 3,000,000 Shares Ar
Traded In Final Hour—The
Tickers Lag 167 Minutes.